This Book Belongs To

_____

"Faith goes beyond the ordinary to help us reach deep into our hearts to appreciate the awe of God. The world needs this now, as so much of the mundane distorts the greatness of our creator God. The questions at the end of each reading are captivating and stay with you for the rest of the day."

MINA BAJOMO, co-founder, Lapis Lazuli Ministries

"I strongly encourage you to accept Faith's invitation to encounter the God of wonders for 40 days through this devotional. Let's shift our mindsets from our normal perspectives to grasping the awe and wonder of our God. Be in awe and be in health!"

DAWNA DE SILVA, founder, Bethel Sozo

"This book provides us with a 40-day tour around the Bible, stopping off at a different experience of awe and wonder at each location. Faith Blatchford provokes us to stop, reflect and imagine ourselves in the story. This devotional will encourage you to see God's goodness in every impossible situation."

TIM ELDRIDGE, Presence Ministries International

"Biblical moments of awe come alive in *God of Wonders*. Each entry draws us into a place where we can truly marvel at God's nature and experience His goodness, holiness and splendor in a whole new way. May we return to a life of being awestruck again and discover for ourselves the God of wonders."

BILL AND BENI JOHNSON, senior leaders, Bethel Church

"Faith is a rare gem of a woman who possesses deep prophetic insight alongside a unique ability to impart heavenly wisdom that goes straight to the heart! I love how this book invites you into core stories, yet at the same time provides great structure and truth. Some of the stories spoke to the core of my heart and truly elevated my experience with the Lord."

GINA LA MORTE, prophetic voice, author, speaker

"Faith ushers in a vital shift of focus from life's challenges into the wondrous awe of God's glorious provision. As a soul whisperer, Faith artistically magnifies God's compassionate, enduring, supernatural activity in our lives, building for us powerful neural pathways into greater intimacy with Him."

STACEY A. LEMMER, Psy.D., M.S.W, clinical psychologist, Transformation Center, Bethel Ministries

"Faith Blatchford leads us to experience God in ways that renew our sense of awe, deepen the connection to our heavenly Father and expand our hope in a difficult world. Definitely a book I'll return to again."

EDIE MELSON, author, blogger, speaker

"Experiencing wonder is a foundational part of our human and creative experience. Faith has given us a practical pathway to reawaken the much-needed sense of wonder in our lives."

STEPHEN ROACH, The Breath & the Clay creative arts movement

"Faith Blatchford is one of the most encouraging, inspiring and mature leaders I know. This will no doubt be a way for you to encourage yourself in the Lord! Please take this time to saturate in the 40 days of awe in the presence of God!"

DANNY SILK, president, Loving on Purpose; author, *Keep Your Love On* and more

"*God of Wonders* isn't just a devotional, it's an experience of deeper amazement and delightful wonder in your relationship with God. You will be treated to Faith Blatchford's fresh voice as she leads you into a rich encounter with the God who loves you."

LINDA EVANS SHEPHERD, author, *When You Need to Move a Mountain*, *Praying through Your Every Emotion* and more

"Wow, this is a great book for a daily dose of awe and glory. Each day I thought, *This is just what my heart needs!* I know you're going to love your personal journey to encounter the God of awe."

BRIAN SIMMONS, The Passion Translation Project

"Indispensable for those who believe themselves to be in the dregs of life, this book is a written invitation from God to reengage with life yet to be lived—a life of awe and wonder!"

KRIS VALLOTTON, senior associate leader, Bethel Church; author, *Heavy Rain*, *Spiritual Intelligence* and more

GOD
of
Wonders

GOD
of
Wonders

40 DAYS OF AWE
in the PRESENCE of GOD

FAITH BLATCHFORD

Chosen
a division of Baker Publishing Group
Minneapolis, Minnesota

© 2021 by Age to Come

Published by Chosen Books
11400 Hampshire Avenue South
Bloomington, Minnesota 55438
www.chosenbooks.com

Chosen Books is a division of
Baker Publishing Group, Grand Rapids, Michigan

Printed in China

ISBN 978-0-8007-6178-3

Library of Congress Cataloging-in-Publication Control Number: 2020942891

Unless otherwise indicated, Scripture quotations are taken from the Holy Bible, New Living Translation, copyright © 1996, 2004, 2015 by Tyndale House Foundation. Used by permission of Tyndale House Publishers, Inc., Carol Stream, Illinois 60188. All rights reserved.

Scripture quotations identified KJV are from the King James Version of the Bible.

Scripture quotations identified NKJV are from the New King James Version®. Copyright © 1982 by Thomas Nelson. Used by permission. All rights reserved.

Scripture quotations identified TPT are from The Passion Translation®. Copyright © 2017, 2018 by Passion & Fire Ministries, Inc. Used by permission. All rights reserved. ThePassionTranslation.com.

Cover design by Bill Johnson

21   22   23   24   25   26   27   7   6   5   4   3   2   1

To all the
writers,
artists,
composers,
speakers,
dreamers
and *children*
who have challenged me
to live in awe of the
God of wonders.

Contents

Introduction

In July of 2018, a devastating wildfire ravaged 229,000 acres and over 1,000 homes in Redding, California, where I live. The majestic redwoods and sequoias, along with most of the other trees in my backyard, were now either shriveled black twigs or charred trunks with brown-fringed limbs. I was thankful my house was still standing in the midst of such destruction.

The scene, however, stirred a deep sense of loss—loss of what had been and might never be again in my lifetime. One afternoon as I surveyed the burned landscape, deep sadness engulfed me. In the midst of my pain, I heard the kind voice of my heavenly Father redirecting my focus as He said, "Look for the green."

The arborist who came to assess the extent of damage to all the trees helped me find the green as we walked around the yard. He pointed to one of the damaged tree limbs covered with the ashen fringe and said, "Look up there. See the green?" His finger directed my eyes to a little patch, an oasis of life, in the midst of the destruction. I realized then why God had told me to "look for the green." The awe I experienced as I chose to focus on those wisps of green, which had somehow survived the raging inferno, lifted my spirit and reconnected me to my Creator, who gives beauty for ashes (see Isaiah 61:3).

God has wired us for awe. One reason we need circuitry within us for this emotion is so we are able to live face-to-face with the powerful God of glory and wonder. Perhaps you have experienced the results of plugging a 110-volt coffeepot into a 220-volt outlet—fried coffeepot. It burned out because it did not have the capacity to receive more than 110 volts of electricity. That is a picture of what could happen if we are not equipped to connect to such power. Another reason for this pre-wiring in us is that the emotion of awe has beneficial effects on us mentally, emotionally, spiritually and physically.

In the last several years, the scientific community has done research on the emotion of awe.* Their studies reveal numerous benefits from this experience: sharper brain function, better sense of calm, increased connection to others and greater generosity. The positive influence of awe

* Anna Mikulak, "All About Awe," *Association for Psychological Science*, April 2015, published March 31, 2015, www.psychologicalscience.org/issue/april -15, which documents eleven references for a summary of these findings.

on the human body gives promise of wholeness. One test measured the impact of seven different positive emotions (e.g., love) on the immune system, with awe showing the best results. The more awe a person experienced, the lower the level of inflammatory molecules in their body. Lower inflammation means better health. Could this mean that to live in awe means to live in health?

These benefits are another example of the divine design of our body, but they are secondary to the most important reason for our God-given awe capacity: to be able to dwell with Him. The Bible has sometimes been viewed as a book of rules and regulations along with the punishments meted out to those who did not follow the rules. The result has been a religion based on fear of punishment. God's intention is that we come to know Him in all His many magnificent facets, not as a punisher but as a lover. As we do, our thinking changes not just about Him, but also about ourselves and the circumstances of our lives.

As you read, remember that Scripture is a living Word, the record of God's compassionate, supernatural interruptions into the everyday trials of His children, to bring His signs and wonders of encouragement and refreshment. Because of the power encoded like DNA in the written Word of God, it is important that we read each day's Scripture selection to encounter this magnificent God in all His mystery and brilliance.

Sometimes we become so enmeshed in the day-to-day—even overwhelmed, as I was by the fire—that we need someone to remind us to "look for the green." This book can be your reminder. After you read the Scripture and reflection, pause and take a breath as you open your heart in the next section. Slowly read the prayer aloud, listening with your spirit to the Holy Spirit as He echoes the words back to you. Then, like a little child, let your imagination explore undiscovered realms of this region of awe. As you take time to "look up," you may be surprised to experience stunning encounters of your own. The Lord is waiting for you in the wonder.

An Invitation to Come Up

Then as I looked, I saw a door standing open in heaven, and the same voice I had heard before spoke to me like a trumpet blast. The voice said, "Come up here. . . ." And instantly I was in the Spirit, and I saw a throne in heaven and someone sitting on it. . . . And the glow of an emerald circled his throne like a rainbow. From the throne came flashes of lightning and the rumble of thunder. . . . In front of the throne was a shiny sea of glass, sparkling like crystal.

Revelation 4:1–6

"Come up here." Did John wonder if he was hallucinating? Under stress, our minds can play tricks on us. He was on the Isle of Patmos, banished from home because he would not stop talking about Jesus. Patmos is a small Greek island in the Aegean Sea, seven and a half miles long and six miles wide. It was not a destination for tourists but for criminals and political enemies of Rome. Life on the island was a day-to-day survival of the fittest. For John, remembering the signs and wonders he witnessed with Jesus might have been a source of comfort and strength.

And then the voice from above interrupted his thoughts. He knew about heaven. Jesus had spoken to the disciples about going to prepare a place for them in His Father's house. The report from many after the resurrection was that He went up into the clouds. It is uncertain if John had read Paul's epistle to the Ephesians. If he had, he would know that we sit together with Christ in heavenly places. This moment was his opportunity to see for himself. The door was open. He did not need to knock. The Spirit would take him up. What a change of pace from his surroundings and companions.

What would his thoughts have been? He might have wondered if this was real. Maybe he had been in the sun too long and now was dehydrated? Should he respond to this invitation? He did not have anyone he could talk with to get confirmation that he was in his right mind. We do not know what John was doing at the time. He could have been doing manual labor, praying, worshiping or doing any number of other things. Did anyone else receive the same invitation—or was John one of the special ones with an all-access pass since he was the one who leaned on Jesus' chest?

Later John wrote that the Spirit and the bride issued a blanket invitation for anyone to come (see Revelation 22:17). Because God never changes, His invitation to all His children is the same yesterday, today and forever. He leaves the door open and the lights on. Come up any time.

⸻

John may have had several moments of awe. Any time a human hears an audible voice from heaven is a life-changing experience. It is possible the greatest impact came when he returned from heaven to earth, to his prison on Patmos. When we encounter God and His glory, our perspective changes. We will think differently about our life, our surroundings and our problems. Did John look out at the Aegean Sea separating him from his family, and remember his Father's house on the sea of glass? Although he was far from his earthly family, he was close to his Father in heaven.

Imagine If

If you had been in John's position on Patmos, how would you have responded to the voice from heaven? Would you have allowed the Spirit to take you up? It is our mindset about God, and about ourselves in relation to Him, that determines our response. Guilt, shame, fear and distrust can stop us from saying a quick yes to God's invitation to His world of wonder.

PRAYER

Jesus, thank You for being the door for me into the Father's house. I do not want any lie or fear to keep me from experiencing the wonderland of heaven. Holy Spirit, search my heart. Reveal anything in my mind or heart that would stop me from encountering the God of awe.

· · · · · · · · · · · · LOOK UP · · · · · · · · · · · ·

Like John, do you feel imprisoned, cut off or trapped in your circumstances? If the Holy Spirit were to take you up through the door to the Father's house, how would that vision change your mind about your present circumstances? When we encounter the heavenly realm, our perspectives will change even if our circumstances do not.

We are *perishing* for want of wonder,
not for want of wonders.

—

G. K. Chesterton

Breath of Wonder

> Then the LORD God formed the man from the dust of the ground. He breathed the breath of life into the man's nostrils, and the man became a living person. Then the LORD planted a garden in Eden in the east, and there he placed the man he had made. The LORD made all sorts of trees grow up from the ground—trees that were beautiful and that produced delicious fruit. . . . "Have you eaten from the fruit I commanded you not to eat?" . . . So the LORD God banished them from the Garden of Eden.
>
> Genesis 2:7–9; 3:11; 3:23

What did that first breath feel like? Did Adam's body shake and rattle like the bones coming together in the valley of dry bones (see Ezekiel 7:1–14)? Did he cough and cry like a baby at birth? Was the oxygen so rich that he experienced a euphoric high? Did his eyes squint at the blinding glory of God's presence face-to-face with him? Oh, so many questions.

No birth since then has been the same, and yet every breath we take comes from the same source—God. Polluted air may envelop us nowadays, but the breath inside that makes us a living soul is pure and holy. Job said, "The Spirit of God has made me, and the breath of the Almighty gives me life" (Job 33:4). Our first breath is a gift of life from God Himself.

Adam not only had the wonder within but he also lived in a garden of wonder. In the first seconds of his life, all five senses were on overload—seeing, hearing, smelling, tasting and feeling the amazing, overwhelming aspects of paradise. Would it have been too much for him to take in? Have you ever experienced so much beauty all at one time that it was almost painful?

"So what went wrong?" we may wonder. "How could two people forfeit wonderland for a snack?" We should learn from their mistake instead of judging them for it.

Paul's teaching in Romans 1 helps us understand the tragedy of Adam and Eve. He wrote, "Yes, they knew God, but they wouldn't worship him as God or even give him thanks. And they began to think up foolish ideas of what God was like. As a result, their minds became dark and confused" (v. 21). At some point Adam and Eve must have taken God for granted. Otherwise they would not have believed the "foolish ideas" presented to them by the serpent. Our worship and gratitude for the God of wonders greatly influences our thinking.

———————∽———————

Is it possible that Adam's most profound moment of awe occurred the moment he stepped outside the gates of the Garden of Eden? Before that, he had experienced nothing but the glory of God. He had gone from paradise to a desert. Was he struck with horrified awe by the contrast? Did he cry tears of regret as he experienced the magnificence of the Garden looking in from the outside? Maybe he begged God to let him and Eve back in. Perhaps he approached the angel guarding the entrance with distraught pleas for mercy. It is hard to imagine the devastation he felt when he realized the enormity of what he lost because of a piece of fruit.

Imagine If

If you were Adam or Eve, what would have been your moment of awe—your first view of the magnificence of paradise or your last one as you left the Garden? Would the contrast take your breath away for a moment? Do you think you would have wept tears of repentance? Or would your heart have already hardened toward God? Often, loss of what we failed to treasure awakens us to the true value of what we had.

PRAYER

God, forgive me for any time I have taken You for granted, opening myself up to foolish thinking. May I never worship or serve anyone but You. There is nothing I could ever imagine that compares with You. Don't let me believe any lies the enemy tells me about You. Renew my mind moment by moment as I behold Your brilliance.

· · · · · · · · · · · · LOOK UP · · · · · · · · · · · ·

There is good news! You do not have to wait for reconciliation as Adam did. Look up and see Jesus—the Way, the Truth and the Life. His death, burial and resurrection reopened the gates of paradise for us. He—the Wonderworker—is your way back to paradise. Consider what you need to confess to Him today to find reconciliation.

Man has to *awaken* to wonder.

—

Ludwig Wittgenstein

Angel Food for the Weary

> [Elijah] went on alone into the wilderness, traveling all day. He sat down under a solitary broom tree and prayed that he might die. "I have had enough, LORD," he said. "Take my life, for I am no better than my ancestors who have already died." Then he lay down and slept under the broom tree. But as he was sleeping, an angel touched him and told him, "Get up and eat!" He looked around and there beside his head was some bread baked on hot stones and a jar of water! . . . So he got up and ate and drank, and the food gave him enough strength to travel forty days and forty nights to Mount Sinai. . . . There he came to a cave, where he spent the night. But the LORD said to him, "What are you doing here, Elijah?" . . . "The people of Israel . . . are trying to kill me. . . ." "Go out and stand before me on the mountain," the LORD told him. And as Elijah stood there, the LORD passed by.
>
> 1 Kings 19:4–11

Have you ever said what Elijah did: "I have had enough, Lord," or even "Take my life"—until you remembered death and life are in the power of the tongue (see Proverbs 18:21)? God heard Elijah's death wish, but instead of correction He sent an angel to deliver comfort food. This was not ordinary bread and water. It was angel food. There is something about the bread from heaven and the water of life that works wonders.

Elijah needed both. The days leading up to his decision to resign had been life-threatening (see 1 Kings 18:15–24). God was not surprised that Elijah had a meltdown. He knew Elijah was not Superman, even if Elijah did not. David wrote, "The Lord is like a father to His children, tender and compassionate to those who fear Him. For He knows how weak we are; he remembers we are only dust" (Psalm 103:13–14).

When children have tantrums, they are not bad; they are probably tired. A good nap and some food change everything. God sees us as His little children who need their Father. How different Elijah might have felt if he had run to his Father rather than from his enemy Jezebel. His little pout did not disqualify him or hinder God's plan for his life.

God did not waste time by punishing Elijah. We are the ones who believe we need a swat or a time-out for our bad behavior. Once Elijah had his nap, the angel came with more food and instructions to head to Mount Sinai. But he needed more than the nap and the hot bread. God knew what he needed—a face-to-face encounter. God spoke to him and said, "Go out and stand before me on the mountain" (1 Kings 19:11). Although Elijah was still complaining and full of excuses, his face-to-face with God got him back on course (see 1 Kings 19:19–21).

Elijah needed more than one moment of awe to change his attitude. God knew Elijah's temperament. One mind-boggling encounter with the Lord of Hosts might be enough for some, but not for Elijah. God never runs out of shock-and-awe options to get our attention. If fire from heaven is not enough, then He has an army of angels to send, or He will meet with us personally.

Imagine It

How many angels or one-on-ones with God would it have taken to get you out of a pout? Do you think one angel feather landing beside you would be enough to shake you out of stinking thinking? Or would it take an angel himself? If Elijah had remained in awe when the fire fell on the altar, he might have avoided the meltdown. In the heat of the moment, he took his eyes off God and his mind convinced him to run and hide.

PRAYER

God, help me to remain in awe. Forgive me for allowing myself to get sidetracked. Thank You for remembering that I am dust. I often forget that. Please continue to woo my eyes back to Your face. When I look at You, everything changes. All the pieces of my mind come together as I bask in Your love and power.

· · · · · · · · · · · · · · LOOK UP · · · · · · · · · · · · · ·

The normal Christian life is power, love and a sound mind. You do not need to be afraid of exhaustion, fear or confusion. One glimpse of God's beauty is enough to restore you. You may not be able to see or feel Him right now. Don't worry. Instead, take a moment to remember a few divine encounters from the past. As you reconnect with those experiences, be refreshed! He is the same yesterday, today and forever even in your memories.

Wonder interprets life through the eyes of eternity while enjoying the *moment*, but never lets the moment's revision exhaust the *eternal*.

—

Ravi Zacharias

Awesome Terror

> When Noah was 600 years old, on the seventeenth day of the second month, all the underground waters erupted from the earth, and the rain fell in mighty torrents from the sky. The rain continued to fall for forty days and forty nights. Everything that breathed and lived on dry land died. . . . The only people who survived were Noah and those with him in the boat. Then God said, "I am giving you a sign of my covenant with you and with all living creatures, for all generations to come. I have placed my rainbow in the clouds. It is the sign of my covenant with you and with all the earth. . . . Never again will the floodwaters destroy all life."
>
> Genesis 7:11-12, 22-23; 9:12-15

Does your dog or cat tremble during a thunderstorm—or even run away and hide under the bed? You may be thinking, "What does a pet have to do with Genesis 9?" A lot, actually. None of those dogs, cats, rhinos, parakeets and other animals on the ark had ever experienced such close fellowship on a boat in the midst of an end-of-the-world flood. This was the perfect storm for a cacophony of fleeing, shaking, howling, screaming creatures. As the "captain" of the ship, Noah must have been bombarded with endless questions from his family. "Where will we live?" "What will we do?" "Are you sure you heard God?" "Why did you think you could trust Him?"

Yes, why did Noah trust God enough to obey Him?

Noah trusted God because he had faith in Him. The more important fact is that God trusted Noah because Noah's thoughts were not evil like everyone else's. Noah's thinking empowered him to be righteous, and God established a covenant with him (see Genesis 6:5–9). This story is a reminder to us of how our belief about God impacts our actions. Solomon wrote that "as he thinks in his heart, so is he" (Proverbs 23:7 NKJV).

Despite living in a culture that had turned against God, Noah chose to honor Him. Noah was not even saved, yet God talked to him (see Genesis 6:13).

•————————∽————————•

According to *Webster's New College Dictionary*, "awe refers to a feeling of fearful or profound respect or wonder inspired by the greatness, superiority, grandeur, etc. of a person or thing and suggests an immobilizing effect."* We have to wonder if Noah's respect for God soon turned to fear or even terror. The Genesis account of the deluge refers to "mighty torrents" of rain (Genesis 7:11). It is possible that wind, thunder and lightning punctuated the pounding rain.

---

* *Webster's New World College Dictionary*, 4th edition (New York: Houghton Mifflin Harcourt, 2004), 99.

Noah certainly had no previous experience with an end-of-the-world storm. Although he may have been trembling with fear along with some of the animals, he was bound to be flooded with even greater awe of God—awesome terror.

Imagine If

How would you have felt after day five or six on the ark? What tolerance would you have had for the stench? We have no details about the plumbing for the ark, but the air must have been rank with animal—and possibly human—waste. Would fear and claustrophobia have made you beg God to let you die like the rest of the world just had? Our degree of trust in God's love for us determines how much of His dramatic displays we can stand.

PRAYER

God, increase my confidence in Your trustworthiness so that, no matter what, I will not "jump ship." Forgive me for any time that I have believed You were against me and not for me. Thank You for the rainbow of promise. May every rainbow I see remind me that I am Your child, adopted by Your love through Jesus Christ.

· · · · · · · · · · · · LOOK UP · · · · · · · · · · · ·

Are you experiencing a storm right now? Do you wonder if you will survive? It may be tempting to give in to panic. Before you do, take a minute to be still and allow God to calm your mind, your emotions and your body. Remember Noah. God was faithful to him, an unsaved man. He will certainly be faithful to you, His dear child who is saved by the blood of Christ. Behind those storm clouds is another rainbow. Keep watching for it.

A core *fundamental* of human existence is wonder—and its analogue is *fear.* You can't have one without the other, flip sides of the coin.

—

Mark Frost

The Freedom of Nothing Hidden

Jesus, tired from the long walk, sat wearily beside the well about noontime. Soon a Samaritan woman came to draw water and Jesus said to her, "Please give me a drink." . . . The woman was surprised, for Jews refuse to have anything to do with Samaritans. She said to Jesus, "You are a Jew, and I am a Samaritan woman. Why are you asking me for a drink?" Jesus replied, "If you only knew the gift God has for you and who you are speaking to, you would ask me, and I would give you living water." . . . "Please, sir," the woman said, "give me this water!" "Go and get your husband," Jesus told her. "I don't have a husband." Jesus said, "You're right! You don't have a husband—for you have had five husbands, and you aren't even married to the man you're living with now. . . ." The woman left her water jar beside the well and ran back to the village, telling everyone, "Come see a man who told me everything I ever did!"

John 4:6-7, 9-10, 15-18, 28-29

Gulp. As you read this passage, do you cringe for the Samaritan woman? The normal response for just about anyone would be to run. From her perspective, the whole encounter was shocking. Jews did not associate with Samaritans. And yet there Jesus was, in Sychar, a town in Samaria, talking with her—a woman He had never met before—and asking her for water. The disciples were more amazed that He was talking in public with a woman. Jewish tradition forbade a man to speak in public with even his sister, wife or daughter. He was not only speaking to a woman, but a Samaritan woman.

It is unlikely that any stranger knew the details of the woman's past like Jesus did. The woman was already in shock from the public meeting, and then He exposed all the details of her sordid past. How could she maintain composure and continue to dialogue with Him? The accuracy of His information about her was astounding. His information did not come from an internet search but from heaven. She told Him, "You must be a prophet" (John 4:19).

What else did He know about her? Jesus knew she had looked for love from the wrong people. And He was about to satisfy her thirst for true love forever. The moment He mentioned living water, her heart responded: "Please, sir . . . give me this water!" (John 4:15). He tapped into her deepest desire and then revealed her calling as an evangelist. The people in her town knew her as "that woman." No one, not even the woman herself, had any idea that she would be the woman to announce the long-awaited Messiah.

———————◦∞◦———————

Nothing hidden—all lies exposed. For most people, this would be an occasion for absolute horror, not awe. Instead, Jesus' demonstration of the prophetic amazed her. "Who is this man?" she must have wondered. "Could He be the Messiah the Jews speak of—the one who will save His people from their sins?" Only God could know her completely and still accept her.

Imagine If

Picture yourself as a woman at Jacob's well. You feel awkward because a stranger, a Jewish man, is asking you to draw water for him. Does he have evil intentions? You are alone—defenseless. Then He engages you in conversation and then calls you out and exposes your past. Would you defend yourself with excuses and accusations? Would you flee? Or would His penetrating love draw you closer to Him?

PRAYER

God, help me not to run from the Light. No matter what I have done, help me experience the wonder of living with nothing hidden. You do not change, so I can be confident in Your acceptance. Thank You that as I let go of the excuses and lies, I will discover the truth of my identity and destiny. Help me run to the Light right now.

· · · · · · · · · · · LOOK UP · · · · · · · · · · ·

Do you feel your heart beating a bit faster after praying those words? Yes, the thought of walking through life with nothing hidden is scary; the Bible tells us that people love the darkness (see John 3:19). Take courage from the experience of the woman at the well. As she looked Jesus in the eyes, she saw love. Go ahead, raise your head—no shame—and look at Him eye-to-eye. Let your heart be still, and be awed by His welcoming gaze.

The wonder in our life should always *point* to the *greater* wonder of the Father.

—

Fred Kwan

Stunned by a Towel

> So He got up from the table, took off His robe, wrapped a towel around His waist, and poured water into a basin. Then He began to wash the disciples' feet, drying them with the towel He had around Him. When Jesus came to Simon Peter, Peter said to Him, "Lord, are you going to wash my feet?" Jesus replied, "You don't understand now what I am doing, but someday you will." "No," Peter protested, "you will never wash my feet!" . . . After washing their feet, He put on His robe again and sat down and asked, "Do you understand what I was doing? . . . Since I, your Lord and Teacher, have washed your feet, you ought to wash each other's feet. . . . Do as I have done to you."
>
> John 13:4–8, 12–15

Discipleship Training 2.0 for Peter and his brothers started the moment that Jesus took off His robe and wrapped the towel around His waist. Several of the disciples had seen that robe glowing in the glory of the Mount of Transfiguration and heard the testimony of healing from the hemorrhaging woman in the crowd who stopped bleeding as soon as she touched that robe. They had learned signs and wonders in Discipleship 1.0, but the foot-washing lesson had not been part of that training. Jesus told them they would do even greater works than He did (see John 14:12). They may have imagined themselves doing the "greater works." But foot-washing?

As Peter and the others realized what the towel and basin meant, they may have experienced a moment of embarrassment. Hospitality 101 taught every Jew to wash the feet of their guests when they came into their home. Even if the disciples had not known about this courtesy, they would have heard Jesus rebuke the Pharisee for not providing water for His feet (see Luke 7:44). Would they be kicking themselves when they realized they had failed again?

It might have felt like an eternity to them as Jesus began the washing process. Perhaps Peter squirmed as Jesus knelt before him. Or maybe he jumped at the first touch of Jesus' hands on his feet. The ministry to Peter's feet did more than just remove dirt. Jesus' hands had touched hundreds of people. They were the Holy Spirit's instrument of comfort, healing and revelation. Peter's loving Creator's hands on him could cleanse not just his feet, but his mind and spirit as well.

───────── ∽ ─────────

What was Peter's aha moment? In his dialogue with Jesus before the foot-washing, Peter revealed that he still had a worldly view of rank and protocol. He recognized Jesus as Lord, but in Peter's mind, foot-washing would never be part of Jesus' job description. The experience must have been both wonderful and terrible for him. At what point did Peter realize that to be the greatest, doing the greater works that Jesus prophesied, meant taking the towel and basin as a servant?

Imagine It

Would you have ripped the towel out of Jesus' hands, grabbed the basin and insisted you wash His feet instead? Or would you have, with an internal protest, allowed Him to kneel before you as a servant? Can you imagine what you might have felt as He placed His hands on your feet put the first one into the basin, gently washed away the dirt and then tenderly dried it before immersing the other foot to wash that one? Would cleansing tears have washed your face as He finished washing your feet?

PRAYER

Thank You, Lord, for showing me what it means to follow in Your footsteps of love. Help me move past what I find uncomfortable and do the greater works as a servant like You did. I want my hands to heal the sick, raise the dead, serve the least or wash dirty feet. May every aspect of my life be a sign and a wonder that points the world to You.

· · · · · · · · · · · LOOK UP · · · · · · · · · ·

What situation or relationship are you dealing with today that challenges your thinking about rank and protocol? Invite Jesus to show you what He would do, even if it challenges your comfort zone. It is stunning to witness the power of serving as He did. The meekness of a servant is not weakness when it is empowered by the love of God.

Jesus came to give us life so *unimaginable* beyond anything else that we could ever hope to conceptualize that wonder cannot help but be our *constant* companion.

—

Craig D. Lounsbrough

Pregnant with Promise

> The name of Abram's wife was Sarai. . . . But Sarai was unable to become pregnant and had no children. The LORD kept his word and did for Sarah exactly what he had promised. She became pregnant, and she gave birth to a son. . . . This happened at just the time God had said it would.
>
> Genesis 11:29-30; 21:1-2

Did you notice the first reference cited is Genesis 11 and the last is Genesis 21? Eight chapters devoted to Sarah's fertility issue. Those chapters represent 39 long years of waiting. Today, a woman's "success" is not measured by the fruitfulness of her womb, although barrenness is painful for any couple longing for children. In Abraham's day, an empty cradle was shameful. And then Sarah's hopeful expectation became the silent cynical laugh heard by God (see Genesis 18:12–13). Yes, God hears the pain no one else does, including yours.

Because of famine in Canaan, Abraham fled to pagan Egypt. As a stranger in a land that did not honor the laws of God, his fear was understandable. He recognized Sarah's beauty would attract unwanted attention from the locals. His concern was not so much about her safety but more about his as her husband. If an Egyptian wanted her for his harem, he would have no problem killing Abraham. Posing as her brother made Abraham less of a threat.

Since Abraham had not had the benefit of marriage counseling that would have instructed him to love his wife as Christ loved the Church, even to the point of laying his life down, lying seemed logical. And over the years, the helpmeet wife of the Garden had become more of a slave wife, required to do as the master commanded. Did Sarah experience a tinge of anger when Abraham told her to identify herself as his sister, not his wife (see Genesis 12:11–14)? Many people today, men and women, would have a few unrepeatable words for Abraham. What words came to your mind right now?

Abraham devalued Sarah to save himself. But it would be hard for Sarah not to have thought less of herself anyway, living with the label of *barren*. Society's expectation for her was fruitfulness. She had failed. After ten years of trying to get pregnant, what humiliation to offer her maid's womb to Abraham. At what point did her disappointment with herself and her husband become disappointment with God?

Only God could know the depth of her dissatisfaction, anger, rejection, loneliness and hopelessness. Did He have all her tears in a bottle like David's (see Psalm 56:8)? Does He have yours? He is the same yesterday, today and forever, so He must.

And then Sarah was pregnant. How long did it take before the little kicks in her belly from baby Isaac produced overwhelming awe? She knew, Abraham knew and everyone else knew it was impossible for her to bear a child at her age. And yet it was evident she was growing either a tumor or a baby, as her abdomen protruded more and more. What was the pillow talk now with Abraham, as the delivery day got closer and closer? Did her cynicism hold her emotions in check till she heard the first cry? At some point her mourning turned to joyful laughter as she cradled baby Isaac—her own sign and wonder, the promise of God.

Imagine If

What emotion stirs in you as you put yourself in either Abraham's or Sarah's situation? Both of them faced disappointment with each other and with God. Would you have railed at God, gone into deep depression or tried to divorce your spouse? Few people would hold on for 39 years. Their experience shows the stunning truth that God is faithful to His promise even when we mess up or even give up.

PRAYER

God, thank You for Your unwavering trustworthiness. You do not lie. You never change. Your word is always true. Forgive me for any time I have allowed disappointment or anger to move me from complete trust in You. I forgive myself for my unfaithfulness and receive Your forgiveness. Your faithfulness to me is beyond my comprehension. May I live each day overwhelmed by this revelation.

LOOK UP

What promise have you been holding on to for a long time? Take a moment and fast-forward. Picture yourself holding your promise. Is it a baby, a reconciled family member, a dream job, a spouse or healing? As you see the promise fulfilled, look up and offer the sacrifice of praise and thanksgiving to the One who was and still is faithful.

Let your soul lose itself in *wonder*, for wonder is in this way a very practical emotion. Holy wonder will lead you to grateful worship and heartfelt *thanksgiving*.

—

Charles Spurgeon

Revelation in Wonder

> Then Job replied to the LORD: "I know that you could do anything, and no one can stop you. You asked, 'Who is this that questions my wisdom with such ignorance?' It is I—and I was talking about things I knew nothing about, things far too wonderful for me. You said, 'Listen and I will speak! I have some questions for you, and you must answer them.' I had only heard about you before, but now I have seen you with my own eyes. I take back everything I said, and I sit in dust and ashes to show my repentance."
>
> Job 42:1-6

Have you ever wished the book of Job was not part of the Bible? Have you speed-read through it for your daily Bible reading plan—or did you even skip it altogether because you were going through a hard time yourself? Nothing to be ashamed about if you answered yes. It is a difficult book to read. But so worth it in the end!

We meet Job in the prime of his life—he had fame, fortune and family. Satan saw an opportunity to test God and Job. Did he know something about Job's heart that God did not? Because the report from heaven was "[Job] is the finest man in all the earth" (Job 1:8). Was God seeing the end of Job's life rather than the present situation? Satan discerned a possible chink in Job's pristine armor. With God's permission, all hell broke loose in Job's life. Why did God allow it? This is one of many questions you may have as you think about Job. Some of them will need to remain in the mystery file. Do not get bogged down on the way to chapter 42.

Job might not have made it to chapter 42 if he had listened to his wife, who thought death would be an answer to his trials as well as the family's. Her suggestion was to curse God and die (see Job 2:9). He was the lightning rod in their family. She thought it would be better for her if he died. His friends burdened him with more useless advice. The more they talked, the worse he felt. You may have had "friends" like his. If so, how did you cope with them? Not easy to remain loving, kind and patient with insensitive, unkind or accusatory comfort in your misery.

Meanwhile, God was waiting to pull back the curtain and begin the shock-and-awe show. He knew Job needed to be awestruck. Job did not need more theological arguments, dissertations or someone else's testimony. His head was already full of thoughts about God not based on intimate knowledge of Him. Head knowledge will sustain us only so long in a trial. We are to live by a heart connection to God, which will inform our mind, not vice versa. When the awe of God overtakes us, our thinking changes.

There is no hint of the exact moment when awe struck Job. Any one of the scenes depicted in Job 38–39 could have been the tipping point. It might have been the sound of God's voice booming from the whirlwind (see Job 38:1). Or maybe it was the picture painted by God of the stars singing together (see Job 38:7). The point is that Job experienced the truth of Paul's statement that "the invisible things of him from the creation of the world are clearly seen . . . so that they are without excuse" (Romans 1:20 KJV). Job's encounter with this God of wonders touched his heart and changed his mind—and he repented.

Imagine It

Could you hear your own voice in any of Job's rants? Or did you hear yourself as one of Job's pious friends giving self-righteous advice as he writhed in pain? If you did, do not start condemning yourself. God sees you as His finished masterpiece, just like He saw Job's end at the beginning. If you did not see yourself at all, it might be good to ask God to search your heart as David did (see Psalm 139:23–24). If we do not see a place of need in our life, we will never have the joy of experiencing God's provision.

PRAYER

Yes, God, search my heart. Open my eyes to see Your goodness in all the glory of creation, in every sunrise, moonrise or twinkling star. Forgive me for any time I have entertained thoughts about You that are untrue. I desire to know You more as You reveal Yourself through the wonders all around me.

LOOK UP

You may not be facing any trials today. If so, be thankful and enjoy the season. But take time to expose yourself to works of the Creator around you. As you do, listen for the declarations of God's glory through the birds singing, the waves crashing or the snow falling in the stillness. These encounters are food for your soul, strengthening your heart connection to God to equip you for tomorrow.

We fall on our *knees* in awe of God's *greatness*.

—

Lailah Gifty Akita

The Setup

> A huge crowd kept following [Jesus] wherever he went, because they saw his miraculous signs as he healed the sick. . . . Turning to Philip, he asked, "Where can we buy bread to feed all these people?" He was testing Philip, for he already knew what he was going to do. Philip replied, "Even if we worked for months, we wouldn't have enough money to feed them!" Then Andrew, Simon Peter's brother, spoke up. "There's a young lad here with five barley loaves and two fish. But what good is that with this huge crowd?" "Tell everyone to sit down," Jesus said. So they all sat down on the grassy slopes. (The men alone numbered about 5,000.) Then Jesus took the loaves, gave thanks to God, and distributed them to the people. Afterward he did the same with the fish. And they all ate as much as they wanted.
>
> John 6:2, 5–11

Was Jesus chuckling to Himself as He asked Philip where to buy food for the enormous crowd? Philip took the bait. He assessed their location, available funds and the vast number of people. His calculations, based on the facts, indicated there would be no way to feed the people. He might have even had a moment to question his teacher's mental state.

And that was the issue. He and Jesus were not thinking on the same plane. Natural and supernatural mindsets rarely come up with the same solution to a problem.

For Jesus, the source to feed the crowd was the same as the one to heal all their diseases—His Father in heaven. If the God of signs and wonders is present, there is no difference between multiplication of food and healing of bodies. Anything is possible. But Philip did not understand that he had the same access to the Father's help as Jesus.

Earlier, Jesus taught the disciples to pray "Our Father . . ." (see Matthew 6:9) for all their needs. Philip did not respond to the food shortage with faith in that relationship to the Father, so he felt pressure to solve the problem on his own. He even might have been a little irritated with Jesus for asking him to get such a huge food supply. Even today, feeding five thousand in the middle of nowhere would be a logistical nightmare.

The feeding situation was not a crisis for Jesus. He already knew what He and His Father were going to do. Did He know the lad was going to be there? Or was the boy a plant, part of the prearranged plan? Children are often a catalyst for the miraculous. They live with a nothing-is-impossible perspective until adults around them teach them skepticism. It is hard to believe that the child was the only person with some food. But he might have been the only one with enough faith to believe he would not go hungry if he gave Jesus the five loaves and two fish. An example of a little child leading—this time into wonder.

When did awe strike Philip's mind? Was it a sixth loaf appearing in the basket, or did Philip need to see the leftovers? He might have thought they had miscounted and there were six loaves to start with. But leftovers after five thousand men—plus women and children—ate till they were full? That was not a miscounting of the five loaves and two fish. That was a miracle.

No verse in this chapter indicates that Philip even had a moment of awe. Yet how could that be possible? The people who ate knew they had experienced a miracle and wanted to make Jesus King (see John 6:14–15). He would be the answer to all their economic needs. Were Philip and the others so involved in the distribution of food that they missed the point of the setup?

Imagine If

Whom do you identify with in this story—Philip or the lad? Would you have felt irritation with Jesus or excited to hand Him your loaves and fishes? Why? Several times Jesus used children as an example of humility. It is a child's lack of mental arrogance that opens the door to the kingdom of heaven, where all things are possible. Oh, to become like little children in our thinking.

PRAYER

Yes, God, I want to become childlike, open to the impossible becoming a reality. Forgive me for any time I have allowed skepticism about Your supernatural power to rob me of Your intervention and provision. Please show me any time my adult perspective stunts my growth as a little child.

LOOK UP

Do you have a crisis facing you? In your job, or your family? Do you feel put upon by your boss or a family member to solve the problem? Is it impossible for you to be the answer? Look around, within and without. What "loaves and fishes" do you have to offer to Jesus right now? He is still in the multiplication business. Be childlike in faith. Hand Him the little you have and be in awe as He works His wonders.

Wonder isn't about finding *answers*, it's about becoming more comfortable with *questions*.

—

Leigh Ann Henion

Who Is Afraid of Whom?

> As Jesus was climbing out of the boat, a man who was possessed by demons came out to meet him. For a long time he had been homeless and naked. . . . As soon as he saw Jesus, he shrieked and fell down in front of him. . . . Jesus demanded, "What is your name?" "Legion," he replied, for he was filled with many demons. . . . Then the demons came out of the man and entered into the pigs. . . . When the herdsmen saw it, they fled to the nearby town. . . . People rushed out to see. . . . A crowd soon gathered around Jesus, and they saw the man who had been freed from the demons. He was sitting at Jesus' feet, fully clothed and perfectly sane, and they were all afraid. . . . And all the people . . . begged Jesus to go away . . . for a great wave of fear swept over them. The man who had been freed from the demons begged to go with him.
>
> Luke 8:27–30, 33–38

Have you ever encountered a demonized person? If so, were you afraid? The description of the demoniac in this passage reads like a horror film. The presence of all these demons in one man supercharged this town's atmosphere with fear. The jailors could not keep him incarcerated because his strength was superhuman. Were the jailors relieved each time he broke free? Better to let him rage in the local cemetery than in town. At least his screams could not scare the dead.

The legion of demons must have traumatized the man himself. In spite of their torment, he was able to get to Jesus. The power of an individual's will is greater than a horde of demons. It is possible the demons did not anticipate this close contact with Jesus. Of course, the demons knew who Jesus was. They were afraid of confrontation because they knew what His power and authority could do to them. It is strange to think that a demon of fear was afraid.

Why did the demons generate such fear? Demons want us to fear them because whatever we fear will control us. They controlled the man and everyone in the town. But in a movie when the hero conquers the demons, are you afraid of the hero or do you cheer till you lose your voice? This sounds like a stupid question, right? Of course you applaud the hero. But in this demons-meet-hero story, the hero, Jesus, was more feared than the demons. The townspeople wanted Him to leave the scene. And the now-sane man terrified them as well. Such a bizarre reaction.

Their response reveals their lack of knowledge about God's attitude toward demons versus humans. Jesus came to destroy the works of the devil, not to destroy humans (see 1 John 3:8). John's gospel explains their actions: "God's light came into the world, but people loved the darkness more than the light, for their actions were evil" (John 3:19). They did not know that there was no condemnation for their sins if they came to God's light—Jesus. Because of their lack of understanding about God, the dramatic display of power that should have caused them to run to Jesus caused them to run from Him.

The demoniac might not have realized the magnitude of his deliverance until he saw the townspeople react to him in fear. Or it might not have been until he had a moment by himself with Jesus. No more demons or people screaming at him. Now it was he and Jesus, eye-to-eye. Everything had changed for him, both inside and out. He knew he had to be with Jesus even if that meant leaving everything behind.

Imagine It

Can you relate to the people's reaction to Jesus? Would such a display of raw power against the demons have stirred up fear? Every story in the Bible reveals another facet of God's power and love toward us. Power wielded by love does not need to be feared. Our deliverance occurs when we surrender to His spectacular power regardless of how much the demons scream at us to stop. When we call on His name, He will deliver us. Every time.

PRAYER

Jesus, thank You for suffering punishment for my sins, to secure my deliverance. Forgive me for any time I have allowed the voice of fearful demons to control me instead of the voice of Your love. Thank You for hearing my cry for freedom.

LOOK UP

If you are feeling harassed by the enemy, caught between fear of his torment and fear of God's light, run to the light. Do not listen to the lies; listen to the still, small voice of the Spirit saying, "Do not be afraid." What do you need to confess so you will no longer fear God's presence? Remember, His power to free you is the same as it was for the demoniac thousands of years ago. You are safe in His marvelous light.

There is wonder in *everything*, the only thing you need to change to see it is your *perspective*.

—

Taylor Schake

Bushwhacked by God

> One day Moses was tending the flock. . . . He led the flock far into the wilderness and came to Sinai, the mountain of God. There the angel of the LORD appeared to him in a blazing fire from the middle of a bush. Moses stared in amazement. Though the bush was engulfed in flames, it didn't burn up. "This is amazing," Moses said to himself. "Why isn't that bush burning up? I must go see it." When the LORD saw Moses coming to take a closer look, God called to him from the middle of the bush. "Moses! Moses!" "Here I am!" Moses replied. . . . "I am the God of your father—the God of Abraham, the God of Isaac, and the God of Jacob." When Moses heard this, he covered his face because he was afraid to look at God. Then the LORD told him, "I have certainly seen the oppression of my people in Egypt. . . . Now go, for I am sending you to Pharaoh. You must lead my people Israel out of Egypt." . . . But Moses protested to God, "Who am I?"
>
> Exodus 3:1-11

For Moses this was another ordinary, lonely day in the wilderness tending his sheep. But for God it was a historic day, marked by an ambush through angelic visitation and a burning bush. The scene was Sinai—God's holy mountain. Did Moses know where he was? Was he trespassing on holy ground?

It was too late to check. Suddenly an angel of the Lord appeared, igniting a bush. There was nothing unusual about the bush itself, but when God shows up, the smallest plant becomes significant—but not to everyone. God was watching Moses. Would this flaming bush get his attention enough to draw him closer?

God is always wooing us closer to Himself, whether with angelic visitation, a burning bush or a still, small voice. Moses noticed this was no ordinary burning bush because it continued burning. Amazing! And to his astonishment, he heard an invisible voice from the bush call his name. Scary? Yes, and more so when the voice identified Himself as God. At that point Moses covered his face.

God had a greater purpose with the pyrotechnic display than to wow Moses out of boredom. He does not use His glory to entertain. His purpose is twofold: first, to get our attention; and second, to transform our thinking about ourselves to fulfill our destiny. Sometimes it is easier for God to lead a bush than a human being. The bush obeyed, bursting into flames. Moses hesitated to follow God's command because he did not see himself as God did. It is through bush-burning encounters that we get a better perspective of ourselves in relation to God. When we obey, He brings the firepower to ignite us in the call.

It is possible that the magnitude of God's call eclipsed the awe-inspiring view of the burning bush. Moses' first words were not "Yes, sir!" but "Who am I?" and again "Who am I?" He might have looked around to see if God was actually talking to someone else. He was so undone by the call, he protested a third time, quite a brave move when a moment before he was barefoot on holy ground, hiding his face from God. It is shocking what a bushwhacking by God produces.

Imagine If

Would you have looked for a fire extinguisher, or would this unusual bush have drawn you closer to God? He loves our curiosity about His mysteries. He is the only person who does not tell us to shush when we pester Him with questions. We have permission to ask Him anything. It is through conversation with Him that we discover the answer to the cry of our heart: "Who am I and why was I born?"

PRAYER

God, I give You permission to ambush me anytime, anywhere. Forgive me for any time I have been so distracted by my own thoughts and circumstances that I did not even notice the bush burning beside me. May the next one reveal not only Your power, but also my purpose on the earth.

· · · · · · · · · · · LOOK UP · · · · · · · · · · ·

Are you wondering about your purpose or doubting your ability to fulfill it? You do not need a burning bush to have a conversation with God. Jesus said He was never alone because the Father was always with Him. And He is with you right now. Ask Him why He has confidence in you. His answer may change your view of yourself as well as Him.

There is a *voice* of wonder and amazement inside all of us; but we grow to realize we can no longer hear it, and we live in *silence*. It isn't that God stopped speaking; it is that our lives became *louder*.

—

Mike Yaconelli

Awestruck by Breaking Nets

"Master," Simon replied, "we worked hard all last night and didn't catch a thing. But if you say so, I'll let the nets down again." And this time their nets were so full of fish they began to tear! A shout for help brought their partners in the other boat and soon both boats were filled with fish and on the verge of sinking. When Simon Peter realized what had happened, he fell on his knees before Jesus and said, "Oh, Lord, please leave me—I'm such a sinful man." For he was awestruck by the number of fish they had caught, as were the others with him.

Luke 5:5-9

For Peter, fishing was not something he did on the weekend to relax with his buddies. No, this was work—hard work. He and his friends had been up all night throwing out their nets for fish, only to haul them in empty. No fish in the nets meant no money in their pockets. And that meant no food in their bellies—or in the bellies of their families.

When they got back to shore in the morning, a crowd had gathered to hear Jesus preach. When Jesus finished, He suggested Simon Peter and his friends go out fishing. Peter did not relish the thought of going out again. Surely Jesus had to know that they needed to clean their nets and get some sleep. And what did He know about fishing anyway? He was a carpenter, not a fisherman. Even so, He was their Master. Honor won over exhaustion. Out on the boats they went again.

Did Jesus know Peter's internal protestations? We would think so. It certainly would not have been the first time Jesus knew what was going on in someone's mind. Perhaps He was already smiling because He knew the outcome of this outing would go down in the annals of local fishing history. Peter and the others kept rowing, unprepared for what was about to happen when they let down their nets.

What joyous chaos must have abounded as thousands of fish eyes stared at them from the decks of the boats. When God works His wonders in our midst, there is always extravagant abundance—plenty for everyone, and then some. He does not skimp. There were so many fish flopping around that the boats were about to sink. What a day. The economic impact of this one-day haul was stunning. Jesus knew a bit more about the fishing business than Peter or the others realized.

For Peter and his buddies, did the awe strike when they saw the number of fish caught under Jesus' direction? Jesus was now not only their spiritual teacher but also their business coach. Up to that point, they may have had a separation in their thinking, between the secular and the sacred. Fishing was in the realm of the secular; discipleship under Jesus was the sacred. That mindset was obliterated as a result of the miraculous fishing expedition. Having Jesus in their life meant having Jesus in every aspect of it. They could trust Him with their business as well as their souls.

Imagine If

Have you ever had to work all night, only to have your boss ask you to work another shift the next day as well? Or maybe you have had the boss tell you how to do your job. Irritating. If you were Peter, would you have yielded to Jesus' request to go out again? And would you have had any expectation of catching any fish under His direction?

PRAYER

Jesus, I never want to miss one of Your marvels because I think I know more than You or that You are not interested in every aspect of my life. Forgive me for any time I have overridden Your direction with my ideas or discomfort in the moment. I want my life to line up with Your commands even if my thoughts are not in sync with Yours yet. Help me remember that Your wisdom always means a boatload of goodness for me.

· · · · · · · · · · · · · · · LOOK UP · · · · · · · · · · · · ·

Think about the empty nets you have in your business. Jesus wants you to succeed, and He also knows what you need to achieve success. Take a moment to ask Him where you should throw your "nets." He knows all the whos, whats, wheres and whens of your business. Invite Him to work His wonders with you in your work.

Even in the *familiar* there can be
surprise and wonder.

—

Tierney Gearon

Escape through the Sea

Then the LORD told [Moses], "I have certainly seen the oppression of my people in Egypt. I have heard their cries." . . . God did not lead them along the main road. . . . God led them in a roundabout way through the wilderness toward the Red Sea. . . . Then the LORD gave these instructions: "Order the Israelites to turn back and camp by . . . the sea. . . . Then Pharaoh will think, 'The Israelites are confused.' . . . I have planned this in order to display my glory." . . . As Pharaoh approached, the people of Israel panicked. . . . They cried out to the LORD, and they said to Moses, "Why did you bring us out here to die in the wilderness? . . . It's better to be a slave in Egypt than a corpse in the wilderness." . . . Then Moses raised his hand over the sea, and the LORD opened up a path through the water. . . . When the people of Israel saw the mighty power that the LORD had unleashed against the Egyptians, they were filled with awe before Him. They put their trust in the LORD and in His servant Moses.

Exodus 3:7; 13:17-18; 14:1-4, 10-12, 21, 31

T he Lord heard their cry. He told Moses He was aware of their suffering. It is hard to believe that Moses did not tell the people that God heard their anguish and planned to deliver them. God authorized Moses to tell Pharaoh and the people that "I AM" commissioned him as the leader. What more did they need to know? God Himself intended to save them from slavery. This was not Moses' plan—it was God's. No need to worry or fear. How could it fail? For the first time in their lives, they could dream of a life of freedom in the Promised Land.

The night of their deliverance was traumatizing. The deafening sound of wailing Egyptians, grieving the death of their firstborn, filled the darkness. As they departed, everyone expected to take the main road out of town, the quickest route to their destination. But God's pillar of light led them into the wilderness. What must the Israelites have thought? "Does He not know this will take forever?" "We will not have enough food for such a long trip." Then once they accepted the route, God changed it. You can imagine the protests. "What are we doing turning around?" "We knew it. We are going to die!"

The change of direction put them up against a wall of water and a sea of Egyptians with horses and chariots about to overtake them. Meanwhile, the Israelites were on foot. Great planning, God! By this time, waves of panic washed over them. At this point their desperate cries might have been, "God? What God?" A return to Egypt looked better to them than this terrifying situation with an inexperienced leader led by a God who did not know the roads.

The highway through the Red Sea had not been enough to awaken awe. Panic still gripped the Israelites' minds because the Egyptians were right behind them. But as they watched the water drown their enemies, they were finally convinced of His might as their Deliverer. Running from the Egyptians had made them breathless; now God's marvelous display of power took their breath away again. He had heard their cry.

Imagine If

At what point in this liberation would you have wondered if it might have been better to stay put in Egypt? Could you have trusted Moses enough to follow him into the wilderness, knowing there was a better route? When would you have stopped believing God had a plan for your life and not just your death? In such a crisis, belief that He not only hears your cry but also loves you may be your pillar of fire through the wilderness.

PRAYER

God, thank You for the assurance from Your Word that You do hear my cries and will save me. Even if the road to freedom takes longer than I hoped and leads me through a wilderness, I will trust You. Forgive me for any time I have complained or questioned Your wisdom. You are my "I AM" on this journey.

· · · · · · · · · · · · · LOOK UP · · · · · · · · · · · · ·

You may be up against a wall with enemies breathing down your neck. You have cried out to God, but it does not seem like He heard you, because nothing has changed. Things may have even gotten worse. Be still a minute. Quiet your heart. Take a deep breath. Remember the Israelites and be reassured in your mind that He has heard your cry too.

As we wait and pray, God *weaves* His story and creates a wonder. We are learning to watch for the story to *unfold,* to wait for the wonder.

—

Paul E. Miller

Marvel of Odorless Smoke

> Nebuchadnezzar said to them, "Is it true, Shadrach, Meshach, and Abednego, that you refuse to serve my gods or to worship the gold statue I have set up? I will give you one more chance to bow down and worship . . . but if you refuse, you will be thrown immediately in the blazing furnace." [They] replied . . . "If we are thrown into the blazing furnace, the God whom we serve is able to save us." . . . Nebuchadnezzar . . . commanded that the furnace be heated seven times hotter than usual. . . . "Look!" Nebuchadnezzar shouted. "I see four men, unbound, walking around in the fire unharmed! And the fourth looks like a god!" . . . Then the high officers, officials, governors, and advisers crowded around them and saw that the fire had not touched them. Not a hair on their heads was singed, and their clothing was not scorched. They didn't even smell of smoke! . . . Then Nebuchadnezzar said . . . "There is no other god who can rescue like this!"
>
> Daniel 3:14-15, 17, 19, 25, 27, 28-29

R eading these few verses may cause your heart to beat faster as you picture the confrontation between raging Nebuchadnezzar and the young men. Would they cave under the pressure? Had they seen others thrown to their death in the fiery furnace? Were they thinking of their families, or were they terrified of physical pain? But nothing moved them from unwavering allegiance to God. They would worship Him as God even unto death if necessary.

So why would God want us to know they did not need to wash their clothes? This seems so mundane. And yet it was not. If you are outside and see smoke in the sky, you know there is a fire. The smoke gets in your eyes and also in your nose. You smell the smoke. When you go inside, the room will smell like smoke because it got on your clothes. Everyone will know you have been around a fire. You might try to hide where you have been, but your clothes will tell on you. The smell test is the best test of the truth.

———————∞———————

For Nebuchadnezzar, the odorless clothes might have been the most convincing proof of God's power. He might have found an excuse for the soldiers who died attending the fire—perhaps they died and then fell into the fire. There are different degrees of heat from a furnace. Maybe the fire was not as hot as he thought. And the fourth man could have been his own imagination. No one else remarked about this extra person in the furnace. But the odor-free clothing was the ultimate proof to him.

Nebuchadnezzar was God's target. God wanted to free the entire nation from the control of false gods. He kept piling on the signs and wonders until there was a tipping point of awe—in this case, odor-free clothing. It was then that Nebuchadnezzar changed his mind about God. He made the bold declaration there was no other God. His change of mind revised the justice system in an instant. One minute you would burn for not worshiping the golden statue, but now you would burn if you spoke one word against the God who saved the young men—and their clothes—from the fire.

Imagine If

There is no point in wondering what you would have done in the situation. You will never know the strength of your commitment until you face the test. All you can do is pray that God's grace will empower you in the moment of crisis. In the meantime, the best thing to do to prepare for such a test is to pursue the God of wonders. The more you open your mind, heart and spirit to Him every day, the more unshakable your faith will be.

PRAYER

God, if I ever face such a test, I want to be like the three young men. Right now I am not sure if I would pass or not. But the grace that sustained them is the same grace available to me today. I choose to focus on Your power and not my weakness. I will go from faith to faith and strength to strength believing in You, the God of odor-free smoke.

· · · · · · · · · · · · · LOOK UP · · · · · · · · · · · · ·

Right now, take a moment to focus on a demonstration of His glory. Perhaps in a Scripture you just read, an image of the solar system on your screensaver or the sight of your baby asleep. The longer you pause and encounter His handiwork, the stronger your faith will be. Allow His wonders to work in you.

Wonder or radical *amazement* is the
chief characteristic of the religious man's
attitude toward history and nature.

———

Abraham Heschel

It Is All about the Tone

> Later that day, after it grew dark, Jesus said to his disciples, "Let's cross over to the other side of the lake." After they had sent the crowd away, they shoved off from the shore with him, as he had been teaching from the boat, and there were other boats that sailed with them. Suddenly, as they were crossing the lake a ferocious tempest arose, with violent winds and waves that were crashing into the boat until it was all but swamped. But Jesus was calmly sleeping in the stern, resting on a cushion. So they shook him awake, saying, "Teacher, don't you even care that we are all about to die!" Fully awake, he rebuked the storm and shouted to the sea, "Hush! Calm down!" All at once the wind stopped howling and the water became perfectly calm. . . . They were overwhelmed with fear and awe and said to one another, "Who is this man who has such authority that even the wind and waves obey him?"
>
> Mark 4:35–39, 41 TPT

Has a terrified child ever awakened you from a sound sleep? Your first response probably was not to shout, "Shut up! Don't bother me again!" You might have been a little disoriented at first, but soon compassion kicked in. Your child might have wanted to get in bed with you or grabbed your hand, urging you to come deal with the source of the fear. Your child needed to know you cared and that he or she was safe. Rebuke was not appropriate.

In this story, Jesus modeled His Father—God. He told Philip, "Anyone who has looked at me has seen the Father" (John 14:9 TPT). Unfortunately, sometimes we do not associate the words and actions of Jesus with the Father. We view God and Jesus as separate beings who play "good cop/ bad cop" with us, with Jesus representing the good one and the Father the bad one. If you read these verses too fast, you might think Jesus was responding to the disciples in a harsh tone as an angry father. They woke Him up in a panic and the next words are "He rebuked . . ." Did the word *rebuke* trigger you? Next we are told that He rebuked the wind and told the waves to be silent—not the disciples.

Once they were safe, Jesus asked why they were afraid. It would be wonderful if we had the video version of this passage. What was the tone of His voice and the look in His eyes? Were His words now a rebuke to them? Was He irritated? Or was the deep love of the Father for His "little children" conveyed as He attended to their emotional needs? We will wonder unless we believe our heavenly Father's nature is always gentle and kind.

⸺⸺∞⸺⸺

According to these verses, the power Jesus demonstrated shocked the disciples. It was dark and they were in an open boat. They had been through what a meteorologist today might call a hurricane. Now they saw their Teacher's words exert more force than the howling wind and tumultuous waves. Their amazement became holy fear: "Who is this man?" As their training continued, they would learn more about the Father's love—the force behind all the displays of power demonstrated by Jesus.

Imagine If

If you had been in the storm, would you have felt confident enough to maneuver the boat to the other side of the lake? Or would your screams for help have roused Jesus from sleep? If you had not acted like God's person of faith and power in the moment, how would you have felt about yourself? Embarrassed you woke Him up? Mad at yourself for behaving like a coward? What tone of voice do you think Jesus would have had toward you?

PRAYER

Jesus, help me hear Your true tone of voice, not the one I hear through my own filters. Thank You for seeing me as a "little child," still in need of a parent's patient love and care. I am so thankful I can always scream to You for help in one of life's storms. I do not need to fear rebuke from You.

· · · · · · · · · · · · LOOK UP · · · · · · · · · · · ·

Are you disappointed with yourself because you panicked in a storm? Have you been waiting for a scolding from God? Guess what? There will not be one. The only reprimand you will hear originates from your own thoughts and the mean barbs from the enemy. Don't listen to either source. Instead, follow the encouraging word from Hebrews: "So now we come boldly and freely to where love is enthroned, to receive mercy's kiss and discover the grace we urgently need to strengthen us in our time of weakness" (Hebrews 4:16 TPT). God's response will astound you.

What was wonderful about *childhood* is that
anything in it was wonder. It was not merely a world
full of *miracles*; it was a miraculous world.

—

G. K. Chesterton

To See or Not to See

The king of Aram became very upset. . . . The report came back: "Elisha is at Dothan." So one night the king of Aram sent a great army with many chariots and horses to surround the city. When the servant of the man of God got up, there were troops, horses and chariots everywhere. "Oh, sir, what will we do now?" . . . "Don't be afraid! For there are more on our side than on theirs!" Then Elisha prayed, "O LORD, open his eyes and let him see!" The LORD opened the young man's eyes, and when he looked up, he saw that the hillside around Elisha was filled with horses and chariots of fire. As the Aramean army advanced toward him, Elisha prayed, "O LORD, please make them blind." So the LORD struck them with blindness as Elisha had asked. . . . As soon as the [Aramean army] had entered Samaria, Elisha prayed, "O LORD, now open their eyes and let them see." So the LORD opened their eyes.

2 Kings 6:11–20

Have you ever been in a crisis at work with an in-experienced employee? Not much help and not safe if he or she panics. There is usually not time to bring the person up to speed or deal with their meltdown. Elisha had access to supernatural help to address his new employee's fear. He demonstrated wisdom as a leader by praying for his servant. He also knew the power of seeing the situation firsthand rather than hearing about it. Better for his servant to "see" the friendly chariots himself than depend on Elisha to tell him they were there.

What would the servant have thought as he saw the hillside filled with God's horses and chariots of fire? There is no mention of the sound of their arrival. They "appeared" to him out of nowhere. Elisha knew they were there but had not informed the servant. The servant's fear made Elisha realize the young man was not seeing what he saw. Elisha needed to train his servant to "see" supernaturally. Soon after God opened his eyes, the young man then witnessed God answering Elisha's prayer to blind the eyes of the Arameans. They all lost their vision immediately at the same moment—blinded in a flash. Elisha then led the blind enemy Arameans on a hike to Samaria. Once there, he prayed again, asking God to open their eyes. Vision restored.

•————————∽————————•

How many eye openings and closings did it take before the servant's jaw dropped? The servant must have thought, "Who is this God that responds to the bold prayer of a mere human? Is this Elisha's God?" Was he jealous of Elisha's relationship with God? Did he want the same kind of connection? He did not have it or he would not have needed Elisha to ask God to open his eyes.

Imagine It

What would you have thought about Elisha's relationship with God? Would you have wanted to have the same connection, or would you have been satisfied to be a witness to this display of authority and power? The blessing of relating to God through Jesus Christ means the power of His Spirit is available to every believer, not to only a few prophets like Elisha. The prophet Joel spoke of a day when the Spirit would be poured out on all flesh (see Joel 2:28). We are living in that day.

PRAYER

God, thank You that I do not need to be jealous of anyone else's gifts, talents or spiritual experiences. Forgive me for any time I have coveted someone else's relationship with You, not realizing the same connection is available to me. It is amazing that You want to use me. I do not want to be a spectator of someone else's supernatural life. I want to open blind eyes, both physical and spiritual, by Your power working through me.

· · · · · · · · · · · · · · LOOK UP · · · · · · · · · · · · · ·

The best time to encounter the supernatural power of God in your life is when you are afraid. If the servant had not been terrified, he would not have needed God to open his eyes. God is able to give you vision as well as visions. God has promised you both. Take a moment now and ask Him to let you "see" the chariots of fire with you in the midst of your fear.

I want to remember to *notice* the wonders
of each day, in each moment, no matter where
I am under any *circumstance*.

—

Charlotte Eriksson

Sleeping with Lions

> So at last the king gave orders for Daniel to be arrested and thrown into the den of lions. . . . Very early the next morning, the king got up and hurried out to the lions' den. When he got there, he called out in anguish, "Daniel, servant of the living God! Was your God, whom you serve so faithfully, able to rescue you from the lions?'" Daniel answered, "My God sent his angel to shut the lions' mouths so that they would not hurt me." . . . Then King Darius sent this message . . . "I decree that everyone throughout my kingdom should tremble with fear before the God of Daniel. For He is the living God, and He will endure forever. . . . He rescues and saves His people; he performs miraculous signs and wonders in the heavens and on the earth."
>
> Daniel 6:16, 19-22, 25-27

Daniel's sleepover companion was not Aslan. For those who have read C. S. Lewis's The Chronicles of Narnia series, you might view these lions as Aslan—not tame, but good. Today, most lions we encounter at a zoo appear harmless as they relax in the sun, letting out a big yawn. No threat there. We do not live in a culture, as Daniel did, that used wild animals as a form of torture or punishment. No one considered those animals to be house pets.

Daniel had impressed Darius. But when Daniel continued to worship his God, Darius had to throw him into the lions' den even though he planned to use Daniel in the kingdom. Instead of a peaceful night's sleep, he tossed and turned in torment over his decision. Daniel does not give us much detail about how he spent his night. Did the lions greet him with teeth-bared, terrifying roars or "as faithful dogs might receive their returning master, wagging their tails and licking him"*?

The lions were not friendly for long. As soon as the soldiers removed Daniel from the pit, Darius ordered Daniel's enemies thrown into it. Before the people hit the floor of the pit, the lions leapt into the air, overpowering them and crushing their bones. Only a few hours before, they shared their home with Daniel.

That sight confirmed to Darius that Daniel's God had saved him. He did not survive because the lions were sick or already stuffed. No, they were ravenous, vicious beasts quieted by their Maker's messenger angel. The angel could simply touch the lions' muzzles and release a heavenly *shush* from their Creator. This display of power by Daniel's God changed Darius. He decreed that everyone should fear Daniel's God because He delivers, saves and performs signs and wonders—wonders with lions.

———————∽———————

* Isidore Singer, *The Jewish Encyclopedia* (New York: Funk and Wagnalls, 1916), 428.

In this story, the moment of awe came not for Daniel but for Darius. Imagine the whiplash of emotions as he heard Daniel's first words of life from the pit. In that second, his body, mind and emotions roller-coastered from the depths of despair to the height of elation. His cries of distress turned to shouts of delight. And with his relief came revelation that Daniel's God was the God of all gods. Darius' moment of awe moved him from the kingdom of demons and darkness to the kingdom of angels and light.

Imagine If

If you had been in Darius' situation, would you have been sleepless in the palace, straining for signs of life from the pit? Have you ever spent an anxious night waiting for a life-or-death word about a loved one? How did you feel when you heard he or she had survived? Did you cry, shout, dance, sing, or fall on your knees? How did that experience deepen your relationship with God?

PRAYER

God—Creator of heaven, earth and lions—thank You for this assurance that no matter what life-threatening situation I face, You can dispatch an angel to protect me. Even roaring lions will not eat me. You are the same God today that You were in Daniel's day. Even today, lambs could lie down with lions.

· · · · · · · · · · · · · · LOOK UP · · · · · · · · · · · · · ·

If you have a situation today that feels threatening, take a few minutes now to picture the arrival of one of God's angels. What sign or wonder might He do to shut the mouth-of-the-lion threat? Allow the picture of that angel intervention to settle your mind to bring comfort, peace and worship.

It would be very difficult to draw a line between holy wonder and real *worship,* for when the soul is overwhelmed with the majesty of God's glory, though it may not express itself in *song,* or even utter its voice with bowed head in humble prayer, yet it silently *adores.*

—

Charles Spurgeon

Not by Might

The Pharisees and the leading priests had given Judas a large detachment of Roman soldiers and temple police to seize Jesus. Judas guided them to the garden, all of them carrying torches and lanterns and armed with swords and spears. . . . Stepping forward, [Jesus] asked, "Who are you looking for?" "Jesus of Nazareth," they replied. (Now Judas, the traitor, was among them.) He replied, "I am he." And the moment Jesus spoke the words, "I am he," the mob fell backward to the ground! As they stood up, they answered, "Jesus of Nazareth." Jesus replied, "I told you that I am the one you're looking for, so if you want me, let these men go home." . . . Suddenly, Peter took out his sword and struck the high priest's servant, slashing off his right ear! The servant's name was Malchus. Jesus ordered Peter, "Put your sword away! Do you really think I will avoid the suffering which my Father has assigned to me?"

John 18:3–8, 10–11 TPT

"Don't you realize that I could ask my heavenly Father for angels to come at any time to deliver me? And instantly he would answer me by sending twelve armies of the angelic host to come and protect us."

See Matthew 26:53

Does it seem odd to you that Peter, the fisherman, carried a sword? As opposition and death threats rose around Jesus, had Jesus instructed His disciples to carry weapons to protect Him as bodyguards? Perhaps Peter was wearing it earlier in the evening when Jesus washed his feet. Was he expecting danger that evening in Gethsemane? He must not have been too worried since he kept falling asleep.

Peter might have been clueless about what was going to take place that evening, but Jesus was not. He did not need swords to protect Him. He lived under the kingdom protection announced to Zerubbabel by the angel: "Not by force, nor by strength but by my Spirit, says the LORD of Heaven's Armies" (Zechariah 4:6).

The soldiers and their weapons were no match for the Spirit of God. This invisible Presence in and around Jesus knocked all of them backward onto the ground! Big, strong military men with swords collapsed in a heap, powerless, in front of the one they came to take into custody. Jesus did not have a weapon, and did not say a word. He just stood there.

Did Peter even notice what happened? Maybe he thought the soldiers tripped on something. But everyone tripping and falling down? Perhaps the fight-or-flight response kicked in so fast that he could not process the details of the scene. Peter felt his Master was in danger, so he pulled out his sword. Once again, Peter failed to be in sync with his Master's perspective. Jesus put the ear back, as if it was a detachable part snapped back into place.

——————∽——————

Peter had a lot to process in a short amount of time. He had just seen a dramatic demonstration of God's protection. In that moment his bloody sword might have felt like a child's toy. When did he realize he did not have the firepower to bring a whole group of soldiers to the ground? One ear versus a pile of bodies brought down by an invisible power. He might have felt more insecure than he did when the soldiers first arrived. At least earlier, he trusted the power of his weapon. Now he had to learn to live by the Spirit, not by the sword.

Imagine If

Can you picture the soldiers laid out on the ground? Would you have been more terrified of the force that brought them down than the power of their weapons? Would you still have pulled out your sword to deal with the enemy soldiers? It takes time to learn that "we use God's mighty weapons, not worldly weapons" (2 Corinthians 10:4).

PRAYER

God, forgive me for any time I have trusted my sword more than the power of Your Spirit. Thank You for covering my actions any time I have chopped off an ear. Your patience with Peter encourages me as I learn to live not by might, not by power, but by Your Spirit.

· · · · · · · · · · · · · LOOK UP · · · · · · · · · · · · ·

If you feel unsafe, invite the Holy Spirit to intervene and overpower your enemies by His presence. Picture them laid out on the ground in front of you like the soldiers in the Garden. You are not defenseless. A myriad of angels is ready to protect you. You are not alone.

A man can no more *diminish* God's glory by refusing to worship Him than a lunatic can put out the *sun* by scribbling the word "darkness" on the walls of his cell.

——

C. S. Lewis

Facedown on Holy Ground

> When Joshua was near the town of Jericho, he looked up and saw a man standing in front of him with sword in hand. Joshua went up to him and demanded, "Are you friend or foe?" "Neither one," he replied. "I am the commander of the LORD's army." At this, Joshua fell with his face to the ground in reverence. "What do you want your servant to do?" The commander of the LORD's army replied, "Take off your sandals, for the place where you are standing is holy." . . . Now the gates of Jericho were tightly shut. . . . But the LORD said to Joshua, "I have given you Jericho, its king, and all its strong warriors. You and your fighting men should march around the town once a day for six days. Seven priests will walk ahead of the Ark, each carrying a ram's horn. On the seventh day you are to march around the town seven times, with the priests blowing the horns. When you hear the priests give one long blast on the rams' horns, have all the people shout as loud as they can. Then the walls of the town will collapse."
>
> Joshua 5:13–15; 6:1–5

Was this commander of the Lord's army traveling disguised as an ordinary person? Obviously, Joshua had no idea whom he was addressing. Earlier, God had told him four times to "be strong and courageous" (Joshua 1:6, 7, 9, 18). Joshua had an opportunity to be brave when he encountered the stranger in the road holding a sword. The commander did not identify himself as friend. He was all business. This was not a social call.

Joshua immediately got as low as he could—facedown on the ground. He might have wished the earth had opened to allow him to go even lower. As a military man himself, he understood the need to honor rank. This man's rank surpassed that of any military leader he had ever met, including Moses. Joshua might have experienced a mixture of panic and awe. His initial thought might have been, "Oh, God, what did I do wrong?" The commander's order to remove his shoes made the encounter more intense.

And that is all we know. But did the stranger give Joshua more information? Or was it God Himself who shared the full meaning of the meeting? When generals are planning an important attack on an enemy, they keep the details under wraps. God did tell Joshua that He had given him Jericho, the king and all the strong warriors. Joshua never mentioned to God that they had not seen the king or the warriors because they had no access to Jericho. God proceeded to give Joshua his orders in this operation. Once again, Joshua never questioned the wisdom of taking over a walled city with daily exercise around the walls, blowing a few horns and shouting. He might have been shaking on the inside at the thought of his imminent death, but both Moses and God had coached him to be strong and of good courage, and so he kept quiet.

On their D-Day, as they took a longer walk around the city while the priests blew the horns and the people shouted, was Joshua shocked when the walls collapsed—or had the commander already given him the battle plan? Whether the walls came down by the invisible actions of the Lord's army or by the supernatural power of horns and shouts, it was a monumental display of God's strategic power and authority as a military leader.

Imagine If

If you had been one of the priests assigned to lead the attack, blowing your ram's horn, would you have called in sick? Or remembered you had a funeral to attend? Or would you have already been so awed by tales of God's wonders in the wilderness that you figured God could win a battle with anything, including a ram's horn, so no need to be afraid?

PRAYER

God, I want to be strong and courageous, able to stand still to see Your glory displayed in battle. Help me not to run from confrontation, but to allow You to open my eyes to see the commander of Your army positioned to fight for me, assuring my victory against overwhelming odds.

· · · · · · · · · · · · · LOOK UP · · · · · · · · · · · · ·

If you are facing a Jericho situation today, do what Joshua did: get facedown on the ground. Begin to worship God. Thank Him in advance for the victory He has already promised. His strategy may not look the same as yours, but His will bring you victory.

Happy the soul that has been awed
by a view of God's *majesty.*

—

A. W. Pink

Breathless, Beholding the Beauty

When the Queen of Sheba heard of Solomon's fame, which brought honor to the name of the LORD, she came to test him with hard questions. . . . Solomon had answers for all her questions. . . . When the queen realized how very wise Solomon was, and when she saw the palace he had built, she was overwhelmed. She was also amazed at the food on his tables, the organization of his officials and their splendid clothing, the cupbearers, and the burnt offerings Solomon made at the Temple of the LORD. She exclaimed . . . "Your wisdom and prosperity are far beyond what I was told. How happy your people must be! . . . Praise the LORD your God, who delights in you and has placed you on the throne of Israel. Because of the LORD's eternal love for Israel, He has made you king so you can rule with justice and righteousness." Then she gave the king a gift of 9,000 pounds of gold, great quantities of spices, and precious jewels. Never again were so many spices brought in as those the queen of Sheba gave to King Solomon. . . . King Solomon gave the queen of Sheba whatever she asked for, besides all the customary gifts he had so generously given.

1 Kings 10:1-13

To ask King Solomon a few questions, the queen of Sheba had to ride an ugly, spitting camel for several months on the 1,200-mile journey from southern Arabia.

Too bad she could not have chatted on a video call. She came loaded with nine thousand pounds of gold, which at $1,500 an ounce would be worth over $200 million, besides jewels and rare spices. It is unlikely she depleted her own supply of gold, jewels and spices even if she wanted to impress Solomon.

In return, Solomon gave her whatever she wanted in addition to the normal token gifts. What in the world could she have wanted? It looked like she had everything imaginable and enough money to buy anything she did not have. The grandeur of the palace and all the furnishings took her breath away, even though her palace would not have been too shabby.

So what overwhelmed her as she spent time talking with Solomon? Was it seeing the grandeur of his palace, or tasting the fine delicacies presented on a gorgeous table? Or did she encounter Solomon's God—a God of love? How astute for a pagan woman to recognize that behind all the glitz and glamour of Solomon's kingdom was the glorious God of Israel, who actually loved His people so much that He gave them a king like Solomon to care for them. Was she hungry for something more than another diamond ring or gold bracelet? Material possessions would never fill the space God carved out in her human heart for His love. She had her fill of riches but not the true riches of His love.

Imagine If

Would you have been curious enough about Solomon's reputation to take a journey like the queen took? Think of the hardship, the danger and the length of time with no coffee shop, hot shower or comfy bed. What would have impressed you the most about the trip? Would you have been stimulated by the conversation with Solomon or talking with his chef or interior decorator? Do you think you would have felt discontentment as you compared his lavish lifestyle with your own? Or would you, like the queen, have been stirred by the fingerprint of God on each tapestry?

PRAYER

O God, forgive me for settling for anything less than Your love. Thank You for reminding me that behind all the riches, beauty and wisdom I may see around me is love—Your love for me. Let me see material things from Your perspective. As a man woos a woman with beautiful gifts or flowers or jewels, I realize You want to woo me through beauty. May I be as undone as the queen of Sheba as I encounter Your love.

· · · · · · · · · · · · · LOOK UP · · · · · · · · · · · · ·

Be encouraged. The solution to discontentment or dissatisfaction in your life is one blink away. Stop right now and think of everything you have. Every good and perfect gift comes down from your Father. Be enamored with His love, the source of true contentment. And give thanks for each gift He has already given.

Gratitude bestows *reverence*, allowing
us to encounter everyday epiphanies, those
transcendent moments of awe, that change
forever how we *experience* life and the world.

—

John Milton

Dreaming on a Stone Pillow

From that time on, Esau hated Jacob because their father had given Jacob the blessing. And Esau began to scheme: "I will soon be mourning my father's death. Then I will kill my brother Jacob." But Rebekah heard about Esau's plans. So she sent for Jacob and told him . . . "Get ready and flee to my brother, Laban, in Haran." . . . At sundown he arrived at a good place to set up camp and stopped there for the night. Jacob found a stone to rest his head against and lay down to sleep. As he slept he dreamed of a stairway that reached from the earth up to heaven. And he saw the angels of God going up and down the stairway. At the top of the stairway stood the LORD, and He said, "I am the LORD, the God of your grandfather Abraham, and the God of your father Isaac. . . . I will not leave you until I have finished giving you everything I have promised you." Then Jacob awoke from his sleep and said, "Surely the LORD is in this place, and I wasn't even aware of it!" But he was also afraid and said, "What an awesome place this is! It is none other than the house of God, the very gateway to heaven!"

Genesis 27:41-43; 28:10-17

This was not a deluxe camping trip for Jacob—anything but. If a stone was the only pillow he had, he did not do much planning ahead for the trip. He was on the run because his deception made him no longer welcome or safe at home. He had angered his dad, his brother wanted to kill him and he had to rely on his mother to protect him. Furthermore, he was alone. It is surprising he was able to sleep with so much to process.

Would you have been up all night weighing the pros and cons of what you had done? Although his mother had made it possible for him to get his father's blessing, was it worth the price he paid? The comfort of home now might have been better than the hope of some blessing in the future. He might have regretted listening to his mother. It is possible he was filled with self-hatred, knowing he was a cheat. Or he could have felt clever considering the success of his ruse. He could not have felt too guilty or he would not have fallen asleep on his rock pillow.

———————⌒———————

There were many awe-inspiring moments for Jacob that night. A dream with God talking to us would be enough for some. Who does not want more of those? But it turned out the God encounter was not a dream. When he woke up, he felt holy fear as he sensed the presence of God. We can only imagine whether he was more amazed by what God said to him or by the sight of the ladder and the angels. Perhaps at some point he realized God would have given him the blessing without his mother's suggestion that he use trickery to get it. God's covenant was the assurance that

He would fulfill His own word; He did not need Jacob's help.

Imagine If

Would you have followed your mother's suggestion to swindle, or would you have entrusted your future blessing to God? Would jealousy of Esau have been enough to cause you to take from him rather than receive from God? How would you have felt after the duplicity, as you camped alone with your thoughts? Would God's words have made you realize you could be home in bed, not outside sleeping on a stone pillow?

PRAYER

God, I realize You do not need my help to bless me. Forgive me for any time I have been jealous of someone else or misled to get what I felt should be mine. Thank You for not withholding from me even when I have not trusted You. You continue to reveal the wonder of Your heart to bless me in spite of my behavior. May I live to bless others as You have blessed me.

· · · · · · · · · · · · · **LOOK UP** · · · · · · · · · · · · ·

Do you have promises from God? Is someone else enjoying what might have been yours? Have you wanted to use your own ingenuity to get what you have been waiting for? When you go to bed tonight, ask God to reassure you about His specific words of blessing. He can speak to you as He did to Jacob. He is your dream giver.

Wonder is the starter kit for *innovation.*

—

Tara Lemmey

Twinkle, Twinkle, Little Star

> After Jesus' birth a group of spiritual priests from the East came to Jerusalem and inquired of the people, "Where is the child who is born king of the Jewish people? We observed his star rising in the sky and we've come to bow before him in worship." . . . And so they left, and on their way to Bethlehem, suddenly the same star they had seen in the East reappeared! Amazed, they watched as it went ahead of them and stopped directly over the place where the child was. . . . When they came into the house and saw the young child with Mary, his mother, they were overcome. Falling to the ground at his feet they worshiped him.
>
> Matthew 2:1–2, 9, 11 TPT

> That night, in a field near Bethlehem, there were shepherds watching over their flocks. Suddenly, an angel of the Lord appeared in radiant splendor before them, lighting up the field with the blazing glory of God, and the shepherds were terrified. . . . Then all at once, a vast number of glorious angels appeared, the very armies of heaven! And they all praised God, singing: "Glory to God in the highest realms of heaven!"
>
> Luke 2:8–9, 13–14 TPT

God pulled out all the stops to announce His Son's birth. All of heaven participated. They had waited a long time for this moment and would not skimp on the celebration. How long had the choir been practicing this first rendition of the "Hallelujah Chorus"? Only the residents of heaven know if Handel's famous chorus centuries later was written in the style of the first one.

It is astounding that the audience for this magnificent concert was a few uneducated shepherds. God does not favor the rich and famous if He wants to display His glory. And He does not need a big crowd either. He plays for those who are awake and listening. Hopefully others in the area were awake. This once-in-a-lifetime concert was not one to sleep through.

For such a grand occasion, God decided to pick one little star as the beacon of light directing the wise men. He had so many stars He could have used. What if He had pushed the dimmer switch to "bright" for every star in the sky? Once again, it was a few wise men who noticed that star twinkling in the sky. As students of nature as well as prophecy, they were awake and attentive to the importance of this tiny star. God does not need an epic Hollywood production to wow us.

———————∽———————

For both the shepherds and the wise men, the defining moment was not the sound and light show but Jesus Himself. He was the Star of the evening, not the angels or the star in the sky. It would have been possible for them to miss the point of the sign and wonder of the evening if they had allowed themselves to worship angels or the star rather than Jesus. God's dramatic acts are meant to connect us to Him, not distract us from Him. A sign is always pointing us to something. We are not meant to camp at the signpost.

Imagine If

As you have watched Christmas pageants and sung "Angels We Have Heard on High," did you wish you could have attended the initial event, not a reproduction? Would the glorious harmonies filling the air have been enough, or would this chorus have made you wonder what on earth caused this heavenly visitation? Do you think you would have noticed that one tiny star—although bright, still only one on a canvas of millions?

PRAYER

God, I do not want to miss any sign You post or any wonder You work. Help me to be awake in my spirit to the slightest brushstroke in the sky or softest note in the air. Forgive me for any time I have been more impressed by the show than by You, the Producer. You are not only the reason for the season but the source of it. You are the God of every wonder, and I worship You.

· · · · · · · · · · · LOOK UP · · · · · · · · · · ·

No matter how dark it may seem to you right now, your future is bright because the Light of the world has come. God continues to point us to our hope, whether with crashing cymbals or twinkling stars. Tonight, go outside and look up at the stars. Let them remind you of Jesus, not only the hope of the world but also your hope for today.

The key to a wonderful life is to never stop *wandering* into wonder.

Suzy Kassem

The Law of Love

Afterward, a Jewish religious leader named Simon asked Jesus to his home for dinner. Jesus accepted the invitation. . . . In the neighborhood there was an immoral woman of the streets, known to all as a prostitute. When she heard about Jesus being in someone's house, she took an exquisite flask made from alabaster, filled it with the most expensive perfume, went right into the home of the Jewish religious leader, and knelt at the feet of Jesus in front of the guests. Broken and weeping, she covered his feet with the tears that fell from her face. Over and over she kissed Jesus' feet. Then she opened her flask and anointed his feet with her costly perfume as an act of worship. . . . When Simon saw what was happening, he thought, "This man can't be a true prophet. If he were really a prophet, he would know what kind of sinful woman is touching him." . . . Then [Jesus] spoke to Simon about the woman. "She is doing for me what you didn't bother to do. . . . She has been forgiven of all her many sins. This is why she has shown me such extravagant love." . . . Then Jesus said to the woman at his feet, "All your sins are forgiven." All the dinner guests said among themselves, "Who is the one who can forgive sins?"

Luke 7:36–39, 44, 47–49 TPT

Awkward! Not for Jesus but for the Pharisee. He must have been quite pleased that Jesus had accepted the dinner invitation. Snagging this controversial figure for a private dinner party was a win for him. And then the prostitute showed up. How did she know about this dinner party? And who let her in?

Not only was she there, but Jesus also allowed her to wash His feet with her tears dripping on them mixed with perfume. Did she get that perfume from one of her customers? Disgusting. What a contrast between the Pharisee's horror and the woman's adoration. She might have met Jesus earlier at one of His outdoor meetings. Or perhaps she knew about Jesus and the woman caught in adultery. If she had witnessed His baptism, then she heard from John the Baptist that Jesus was the one who could forgive sin. She was willing to take a risk to meet this man who might forgive her sins—and He did.

•————∽————•

The woman's moment of awe was not the same as the Pharisee's. As she wept, experiencing Jesus' forgiveness, the Pharisee became even more agitated. First the prostitute came to his party, then Jesus showed no discernment about who was touching Him and then He violated the law by pronouncing forgiveness to her. Who did He think He was? God? The woman knew the weight of the law the Pharisee lived by, but in that moment she encountered the power of a greater law—the law of love. Her outpouring of tears, oil and perfume was the measure of both her sin and His love covering it. What wondrous love.

Imagine If

Would the outpouring of His love for the woman have overcome any discomfort you might have felt having this prostitute at your dinner table? Given the danger of crashing the party, would your awareness of your need to meet Jesus have overcome your fear of arriving uninvited? The prostitute did not let the shame of her past keep her from love. But the Pharisee chose to let his rules keep him from it. With whom do you identify? Would His love have overruled your rules—religious, cultural or self-imposed?

PRAYER

God, I do not want to be like the Pharisee. Forgive me for any time I have let my rules and judgments of others or of myself overrule Your love. My past may not be as sinful as that of the woman in this story, but I still need forgiveness. Right now, I kneel before You, pouring out my heart as I open my spirit to receive Your cleansing love.

· · · · · · · · · · · LOOK UP · · · · · · · · · · ·

Is your heart stirred, but you still believe not even Jesus can forgive your sins? Do not despair. The love poured out on the prostitute years ago is still available today. Don't let guilt keep you from gazing into His loving eyes. What do you need forgiveness for? Ask for it. Don't resist for another second— let His love in and be free from shame.

Without wonder, there's no *progress*.
Nothing gets done, nobody goes anywhere. . . .
A civilization without wonder is a *civilization*
that's starting to atrophy and die.

—

Brian Hodge

Unimaginable Night on the Water

> And as night fell he was there praying alone with God. But the disciples, who were now in the middle of the lake, ran into trouble, for their boat was tossed about by the high winds and heavy seas. At about four o'clock in the morning, Jesus came to them, walking on the waves! When the disciples saw him walking on top of the water, they were terrified and screamed, "A ghost!" Then Jesus said, "Be brave and don't be afraid. I am here!" Peter shouted out, "Lord, if it's really you, then have me join you on the water!" "Come and join me," Jesus replied. So Peter stepped out onto the water and began to walk toward Jesus. But when he realized how high the waves were, he became frightened and started to sink. "Save me, Lord!" he cried out. Jesus immediately stretched out his hand and lifted him up and said, "What little faith you have! Why would you let doubt win?" And the very moment they both stepped into the boat, the raging wind ceased. Then all the disciples crouched down before him and worshiped Jesus. They said in adoration, "You are truly the Son of God!"
>
> Matthew 14:23-33 TPT

Peter went from terror at the sight of a ghost walking on the water to such great faith that he walked on the water himself. What happened? Fear paralyzes. It does not empower the impossible, but hinders it. We know from

Scripture that perfect love casts out fear (see 1 John 4:18). God is perfect love, the only perfect love available. Jesus, the embodiment of God's love, who stopped the winds with a word, can also quench our fear with His loving voice.

Jesus never actually invited Peter to take a walk with Him on the water. But Jesus' loving words to be courageous catapulted him onto the water, a place his own mind would have never allowed him to go. He reacted with the mind of Christ, for whom walking on water was normal—not a wonder. But the minute he thought about what he was doing, fear took over and he sank. Without fear, everything is possible—even the impossible! That is why Jesus pointed to a child as the model for kingdom life. Children are open to the impossible because they have not had years of training in fear.

———————∽———————

It was not until Peter was back in the boat that he realized that he, a mere human, had done what no other human had done—walk on water. He might have felt cocky for a minute. But he knew there were certain unbreakable laws of nature that would prevent what he had done. The realization of the difference between his water-walking skill and Jesus' brought startling new revelation that the Master must be God. An encounter with the living God will change our thinking and stir our heart to awe—so Peter and the others worshiped Him.

Imagine It

It is hard to imagine anyone stepping out of a boat in the dark to walk on the water with howling winds all around. Would you have dared? Jesus encouraged him to come once He knew Peter wanted to join Him. Was Jesus delighted seeing Peter's eagerness to do the impossible? He told the disciples nothing would be impossible for them. They were not to tempt God with childish antics, but, if necessary, empowered by the Holy Spirit, they would be able to override the rules.

PRAYER

God, I want to be childlike in faith, believing all things are possible. Forgive me for any time I have allowed fear to rob me of the adventure of living by faith in the Spirit. Open my mind to Your thoughts and my ears to Your empowering voice. I am in awe of the infinite possibilities for me as I walk with You as Your child, whether on land or on water.

· · · · · · · · · · · · LOOK UP · · · · · · · · · ·

Have you recently taken a risk and "stepped out of the boat"? Instead of staying focused on Jesus, did you look down at the waves? Now you feel panic, cannot breathe and are certain you will drown. Stop and remember Peter. He did not drown and neither will you. Extend your right hand to Jesus right now. David said He holds us by our right hand (see Psalm 73:23). Feel His strong grip. You are safe "out of the boat." He has you. Just keep holding His hand like a little child.

To cease to wonder is to fall plumb-down from the *childlike* to the commonplace—the most undivine of all moods intellectual. Our nature can never be at home among things that are not *wonderful* to us.

—

George MacDonald

Shaken to Faith

Then Jesus shouted, "Father, I entrust my spirit into your hands!" And with those words he breathed his last. When the Roman officer overseeing the execution saw what happened, he worshiped God and said, "Surely this man was innocent."

Luke 23:46-47

For three hours, beginning at noon, darkness came over the earth. . . . Jesus passionately cried out, took his last breath, and gave up his spirit. At that moment the veil in the Holy of Holies was torn in two from the top to the bottom. . . . Now, when the Roman military officer and his soldiers witnessed what was happening and felt the powerful earthquake, they were extremely terrified. They said, "There is no doubt, this man was the Son of God!"

Matthew 27:45, 50-51, 54 TPT

Crucifixions were a brutal but normal part of Roman penalty for slaves and insurgents. In 4 BC, two thousand political enemies were crucified by the Roman general Varus.* No telling how many of these the Roman centurions had attended. After some time, one would become numb

* *The New Bible Dictionary* (Grand Rapids: Eerdmans, 1963), 281.

to this gruesome punishment. After six hours or so, once the criminal died, the soldier could go home as if nothing traumatic had happened. This one was different. It would be hard for a soldier not to be aware of the hullabaloo surrounding Jesus and the unusual phenomenon accompanying the event.

Jesus' ministry had stirred up the Jewish leaders to the point that Pilate, the Roman governor, got involved. This year the normal release of a prisoner by the governor during Passover was fraught with controversy. The people, agitated by the priests and elders, wanted Jesus to be crucified and the notorious criminal Barabbas to be released. However, the centurion's job was not to determine innocence or guilt of the prisoner but to make sure the execution took place.

One wonders if his curiosity was stirred by the sign "This is the King of the Jews" hanging above His head (see Luke 23:38). Or he might have overheard the conversation between Jesus and one of the criminals hanging beside Him and wondered what Jesus meant when He said, "I assure you, today you will be with me in paradise" (Luke 23:43). Strange comment. Or perhaps the darkness in the middle of the day seemed strangely different from previous dark storm clouds.

•————∽————•

And then the earth moved. It was not in the three hours of darkness over the earth, but in the shaking, that the centurion knew Jesus' true identity. The Bible records several earthquakes, so this may not have been the first one the centurion had experienced. But was it the first one attached to such an unusual crucifixion?

If you have ever experienced an earthquake, you know they are frightening. But was his terror about the earth shaking or about the One who caused it to move? David wrote: "The earth shook, the heavens also dropped at the presence of God" (Psalm 68:8 KJV). Was the centurion aware of God's presence in the midst of the ground moving under him? Imagine what raced through his mind as he realized what he had participated in.

Imagine If

How would you have felt as the earth was still shaking? Would you have feared for your life, knowing you had participated in the crucifixion of God's Son? Would you have wanted to kill yourself as Judas did when he realized what he had done (see Matthew 27:5)? Or would you have remembered the words of the prisoner next to Jesus? He recognized he was a sinner and asked for mercy (see Luke 23:41–42).

PRAYER

Jesus, You are the Son of the most-high God. May I be as moved by Your presence now as the earth was at Your crucifixion. Break up any hardness in my heart. Forgive me for any time I have not recognized Your majesty as King. Thank You for Your mercy, which opens the door to paradise for me.

· · · · · · · · · · · · LOOK UP · · · · · · · · · · · ·

Do you have a family member or friend who does not acknowledge Jesus as God's Son? Is this person hostile at any mention of Him, creating tension in the relationship? If so, do not despair. The God who brought revelation of Jesus as King to the Roman soldier as the earth moved can do the same for this individual. It may not occur during an earthquake, but all of heaven declares the glory of God. It is only a matter of time until your loved one is shaken to faith. Take a minute right now to ask God to reveal Himself to this person.

The surest way to suppress our ability to understand the *meaning* of God and the importance of worship is to take things for granted. Indifference to the *sublime* wonder of living is the root of sin.

—

Abraham Heschel

Money Meets Its Master

> In the city of Jericho there lived a very wealthy man named Zacchaeus, who was the supervisor over all the tax collectors. As Jesus made his way through the city, Zacchaeus was eager to see Jesus. . . . So he ran on ahead of everyone and climbed up a blossoming fig tree so he could get a glimpse of Jesus as he passed by. When Jesus got to that place he looked up into the tree and said, "Zacchaeus, hurry on down, for I am appointed to stay at your house today!" . . . As Jesus left to go with Zacchaeus, many of the crowd complained, "Look at this! Of all the people to have dinner with, he's going to eat in the house of a crook." Zacchaeus joyfully welcomed Jesus and was amazed over his gracious visit to his house. Zacchaeus stood in front of the Lord and said, "Half of all I own I will give to the poor. And Lord, if I have cheated anyone, I promise to pay back four times as much as I stole."
>
> Luke 19:1–8 TPT

Jesus was famous for His teaching and the miracles He performed, but also for socializing with sinners at dinner parties. It is hard to know which aspect of His fame enflamed the Pharisees the most. It appeared that sinners enjoyed His company more than those who considered themselves righteous. Zacchaeus, a tax collector, might have heard about the feasts Jesus attended, hosted by Matthew, also a tax collector, who left his lucrative tax job to become a disciple of Jesus.

What was in his mind when he climbed the tree to see Jesus as He walked by? Jesus might have already known Zacchaeus' desire. It would not have been the first time Jesus knew someone's thoughts (see Luke 11:17). Tax collectors were often hated and rejected because of their dishonesty, assessing more tax than was legal. Perhaps Zacchaeus just wanted to see this local celebrity, Jesus, from a distance, or maybe he hoped to have a one-on-one conversation with Him. Did he feel the love and acceptance even in Jesus' voice as He called to him?

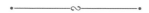

We do not know when awe struck, but at some point it did. Why else would Zacchaeus, a rich man, greet Jesus at the door, confess he had cheated people and pledge to give away half of his fortune and repay people four times the amount he had overcharged? Jesus had told the disciples it was harder for a rich man to enter the kingdom than for a camel to go through the eye of a needle. Yet here was a wealthy man entering the kingdom. The love of money is a strong bond, sometimes difficult to break. What happened to change Zacchaeus? It is possible the love Zacchaeus felt even as Jesus called to him was like a magnet, drawing his love away from money to Jesus. In that moment Zacchaeus saw Jesus as his Master. Both he and his money met the Master.

Imagine If

Have you ever been so overcome by God's love that you experienced instantaneous deliverance? What if you had to make a choice like Zacchaeus? Would you choose riches or Jesus? Jesus acknowledged that is a difficult decision. But He said what might be impossible for a person is possible with God (see Luke 1:37). The secret to God's possibility power is His love. You may have wealth or may have a desire to be wealthy. There is nothing wrong with wanting money. The issue is what do you love. Loving Jesus brings love to us; loving money brings bondage. Who or what is *your* master?

PRAYER

Jesus, I want Your love to be the force that pulls everything into proper order. Forgive me for loving money or the things money can buy more than I love You. Without You, it is impossible for me to live free from materialism. Release Your marvelous love into any area of my heart that loves something other than You.

· · · · · · · · · · · · LOOK UP · · · · · · · · · · · ·

Sometimes money becomes our master through the back door of debt and guilt. No need to despair. God owns all the gold and silver. Since it all belongs to Him, look to Him as the Master of all your money, even the debt. He has a financial plan tailor-made for you—and He will share it with you at no cost. Ask Him to do so today.

Our most precious resource now is wonder. What we wonder about ignites our *imagination,* unleashes our *empathy,* fuels our ferocity.

—

Amy Irvine

Risky Relationship

Whenever Moses went out to the Tent of Meeting, all the people would get up and stand in the entrance of their own tents. They would all watch Moses until he disappeared inside. As he went into the tent, the pillar of cloud would come down and hover at its entrance while the LORD spoke with Moses. When the people saw the cloud standing at the entrance of the tent, they would stand and bow down in front of their own tents. Inside the Tent of Meeting, the LORD would speak to Moses face to face, as one speaks to a friend. . . . One day Moses said to the LORD, "You have been telling me, 'Take these people up to the Promised Land.' But you haven't told me whom you will send with me. . . . And remember that this nation is your very own people." The LORD replied, "I will personally go with you." . . . Then Moses said, "If you don't personally go with us, don't make us leave this place. How will anyone know that you look favorably on me . . . and on your people—if you don't go with us?" . . . The LORD replied to Moses, "I will indeed do what you have asked, for I look favorably on you, and I know you by name."

Exodus 33:8-17

This passage sounds like a conversation between friends, and it was—between God and His friend Moses. Or we could say between Moses and His friend God. Either way, it was incredible that God would condescend to have such an exchange with a human, not even a redeemed one. Moses was either brave or stupid to enter into such a risky relationship.

His assistant, Joshua, went with him, but no one else wanted to tag along when he had these meetings with God. It would be normal for the people to wonder if God would kill Moses if he misspoke, leaving them leaderless in the wilderness. They would have had even more fear if they had overheard their conversation. Moses had the audacity to question God. Did he think God would forget some important part of the plan? Moses even dared to threaten direct disobedience if God did not agree to his demands. How absurd or arrogant. Who did he think he was? It sounds like his role as leader had gone to his head. And yet in spite of Moses' confrontational attitude, God called him the meekest man on earth (see Numbers 12:3).

———∞———

How did this friendship happen? Did Moses grow into this relationship over time? Was becoming a friend of God similar to developing friendship with another human? If we heard the audio of the conversation, would there be some apprehension in the tone of his voice? When did fear give way to trust? At some point, Moses must have received revelation that God was not an unpredictable, angry dictator but a trustworthy, loving friend who, if necessary, would lay His life down for him. Because that is what a friend does, according to Jesus (see John 15:13). And He was the kind of friend who listened to what Moses had to say. It is one thing to talk to God. It is another for God to show that He heard by His response. He agreed to Moses' demand.

Imagine If

How would you have felt at your first one-on-one in the tent with the God who had such power that He created a highway on the sea floor by moving the water into walls? Would you have been quivering, speechless, or both? Would you have pinched yourself to make sure this was real and not a dream? How would you have felt if God acquiesced to your ultimatum?

PRAYER

God, it is hard to believe You want to be my friend. There are so many times I have questions but am hesitant to express my concerns to You. I have no trouble telling my close friends my opinions, and they feel free to tell me theirs. Forgive me for the times I clam up, believing You will be angry with me. May I be as comfortable with You as Moses was, knowing You as my loving friend and not my harsh accuser.

· · · · · · · · · · · · LOOK UP · · · · · · · · · · · ·

You may have one friend or many. Would it not be incredible to add God to your friend list? There may be a lot of reasons you hesitate to initiate the first meeting. Your reasons are irrelevant; He knows them all and does not care. He has been waiting in the tent to meet with you since before you were even born. Run to Him right now with childlike trust. Talk to your Friend.

> When God is our Holy Father, *sovereignty,*
> holiness, omniscience . . . do not terrify us;
> they leave us full of awe and *gratitude.*
>
> —
>
> Ravi Zacharias

The Cloud in the House

So Solomon finished all his work on the Temple of the LORD. . . . The trumpeters and singers performed together in unison to praise and give thanks to the LORD. . . . At that moment a thick cloud filled the Temple of the LORD. The priests could not continue their service because of the cloud, for the glorious presence of the LORD filled the Temple of God. . . . Then Solomon prayed, "O LORD, you have said that you would live in a thick cloud of darkness. Now I have built a glorious Temple for you, a place where you can live forever!" . . . When Solomon finished praying, fire flashed down from heaven and burned up the burnt offerings and sacrifices, and the glorious presence of the LORD filled the Temple. The priests could not enter the Temple of the LORD because the glorious presence of the LORD filled it. When all the people of Israel saw the fire coming down and the glorious presence of the LORD filling the Temple, they fell face down on the ground and worshiped and praised the LORD, saying, "He is good! His faithful love endures forever!"

2 Chronicles 5:1, 13-14; 6:1-2; 7:1-3

Solomon and the Israelites knew about the cloud. They would have heard the stories of the pillar of cloud leading their ancestors through the wilderness during the day. This was a new experience—the cloud was in the Temple.

God had not asked him to build this, so he had no assurance God would even show up. He was completing the building project of his father, King David, who had amassed enormous sums of money for the Temple. Because he had been a man of war, God did not permit him to build it.

It was a bold undertaking that had taken twenty years to complete. What if after all this work God was content to live in the thick cloud of darkness in the heavens rather than on earth in this man-made house? Solomon had no confidence the people were holy enough for Him to come down for more than a visit now and then. If He did come, it was unclear what they should do. They had no book of etiquette to carry out proper protocol. There might even be special offerings required for a resident God versus a visiting one. It was not wisdom to be unprepared for God's arrival.

———————⌒———————

When did Solomon realize he had fulfilled his father's wish? Was it when God first filled the Temple in the cloud, or did it take a week or a month or years to know God had come to stay and not just to visit? God's desire all along had been to live with His children. Over and over He told Solomon's ancestors He wanted to dwell with them. They did not understand His brilliant plan for reconciliation after the breakup of the family in the Garden of Eden. But at some point the revelation must have hit him that this dwelling place, the

Temple, was God's desire more than his. How astounding that God actually wanted to reside with him.

Imagine It

Would God's arrival have shocked you? Or would you have been nervous when He arrived? We have the benefit of the rest of the Old Testament and the New Testament to be confident He would come. We are not destined to live in a house with no Dad. Finally, Jesus came with the name Immanuel—God with us. What Solomon did not know is that God not only wants to live with us but *in* us. Jesus told the disciples that the Holy Spirit "lives with you now and later will be in you" (John 14:17). Yes, we are to be the house with the cloud inside. The knowledge of this can be the catalyst for a life filled with worship.

PRAYER

Thank You, God, for loving me so much that You want to live in me. You amaze me because I see so many flaws and so much mess inside. Sometimes I do not even want to live with myself, much less have You, God, living in me. Expand my understanding of Your astounding love for me. Even though it is messy inside, I am willing for You to take up residence.

· · · · · · · · · · · · · · · · · **LOOK UP** · · · · · · · · · · · · · · ·

You may think it is possible for others to experience God as a housemate, but not you. God is always standing at your door knocking. Invite Him in. He will not mind the mess. He has seen much worse. Right now, even if you feel a little nervous, say, "Come in. Holy Spirit, You are welcome here in me."

The fairest thing we can experience is the *mysterious*. The true scientist never loses the faculty of amazement. It is the *essence* of his being.

—

Hans Selye

Poetry of the Indescribable

> Lord, your name is so great and powerful! People every-
> where see your splendor. Your glorious majesty streams
> from the heavens, filling the earth with the fame of your
> name! . . . Look at the splendor of your skies, your creative
> genius glowing in the heavens. When I gaze at your moon
> and your stars, mounted like jewels in their settings, I know
> you are the fascinating artist who fashioned it all! . . . All the
> created order and every living thing of the earth, sky, and
> sea—the wildest beasts and all the sea creatures—everything
> is in submission to Adam's sons. Lord, your name is so great
> and powerful. People everywhere see your majesty! What
> glory streams from the heavens, filling the earth with the
> fame of your name!
>
> Psalm 8:1, 3, 7–9 TPT

As a teenager relegated to the back forty with the sheep, I doubt David had any idea that people would be reading his poetry thousands of years later. The future that David envisioned for himself while hanging around sheep 24/7 was probably not that grandiose—certainly not a picture of the "you can be whatever you put your mind to" messages youth hear today. Sounds like a pretty boring existence.

His dad did not see much value in him; he did not even include him in the sibling lineup for Samuel the prophet (see 1 Samuel 16:10–11). In the end, his earthly father's rejection did not matter because his heavenly Father had already marked him for future greatness. No one but God knew the training camp for this future psalmist-king took place as he lived alone in the field with his sheep.

With no distractions around him except an occasional lost sheep to save, all David's senses could focus on the wonder around him day and night. He experienced the splendor of every sunrise, the fragrance of wildflowers, the feel of tiny raindrops washing his face, the harvest moon bathing the sheep in light and blinding meteor showers displayed on the backdrop of the black dome of heaven. And even while David slept, his Creator visited him and shared His thoughts, sometimes even in song (see Psalm 139:17–18; Psalm 42:8). Those nighttime revelations might have become the lyrics to the songs David wrote. He lived as a prisoner of God's creative exuberance. What a magnificent confinement to enjoy.

•———————∞———————•

David's every waking moment would be a living synonym of awe. The important moment would be the one when he reached his intake limit. At the splendor-overload point, David must have burst into song or scratched his first poem with whatever he could find for pen and paper. It was not about good grammar or perfect pitch. He had to release the wonderment even though his words could never describe such indescribable glory. The heavens did a better job than he ever could, but that did not stop him. He was not trying to compete. He was willing to collaborate and allow the wonder to guide his pen.

Imagine It

If you had been in David's situation, what outlet would you have found when you could not take in any more magnificence? It does not appear David had formal training as a poet or musician, but when he encountered God's handiwork, he also tapped into his Creator. The gifts and talents within him came alive, awakened by connection with the Creator. Who knows what undiscovered creativity would burst out of you. David had no idea of the impact of his creative expression, and who knows the influence of your pen or instrument in the years to come.

PRAYER

God, thank You for the gifts and talents within me, even those I have not discovered yet. Forgive me for any time I have quenched creative expression through fear or comparison. I may not be a David to the world, but for the sake of the world, I want to be all You created me to be. May I hear the heavens declare Your glory and release my voice to echo their song.

· · · · · · · · · · · LOOK UP · · · · · · · · · · ·

You may have found your voice and already started giving expression through writing, music or art. But are you feeling stuck at the moment? Do you wonder if you will ever get unstuck? The answer to this second question is yes. Or you may not even have been able to start expressing yourself. The antidote to both situations is to overdose on beauty. Get so filled up by going for a walk in the woods or strolling through an art museum that you will burst if you do not express your feelings. Let the creative expression begin today.

Thank God I have seen an orange sky with purple clouds. How easy it is to forget that we have the *privilege* of living in God's art gallery.

—

Erica Goros

Amazing Faith

At that time the highly valued slave of a Roman officer was sick and near death. When the officer heard about Jesus, he sent some respected Jewish elders to ask him to come and heal his slave. So they earnestly begged Jesus to help the man. "If anyone deserves your help, he does," they said, "for he loves the Jewish people and even built a synagogue for us." So Jesus went with them. But just before they arrived at the house, the officer sent some friends to say, "Lord, don't trouble yourself by coming to my home, for I am not worthy of such an honor. I am not even worthy to come and meet you. Just say the word from where you are, and my servant will be healed. I know this because I am under authority of my superior officers, and I have authority over my soldiers. I only need to say, 'Go,' and they go, or 'Come,' and they come." When Jesus heard this, he was amazed. Turning to the crowd that was following him, he said, "I tell you, I haven't seen faith like this in all Israel!" And when the officer's friends returned to his house, they found the slave completely healed.

Luke 7:2-10

Were the disciples perplexed when Jesus headed to the Roman soldier's home to heal his slave? There was such a demand on Jesus, and only so many hours in a day. Did people have no respect? If He did not disappear at night to the mountain to pray, they would have expected Him to minister day and night. Furthermore, did this slave deserve such personal attention? Could Jesus not send two of them instead of going Himself? The disciples still had a lot to learn about the way Jesus operated. They still made decisions based on their human understanding rather than divine revelation.

Jesus, on the other hand, did not act from His head but from His heart—a heart of compassion. Matthew reported that Jesus healed the sick He saw in the midst of a great multitude because "he was moved with compassion toward them" (Matthew 14:14 NKJV). His kind response to a person's pain, suffering and desperation was never based on their social or military rank, material wealth or even their great faith. Jesus said a mustard seed of faith was enough to move a mountain (see Matthew 17:20), so it would certainly be enough to heal the soldier's slave.

The Roman centurion's faith impressed the disciples. Jesus was so amazed, He said He had never seen such faith in the entire kingdom of Israel. That was quite a statement. Did the disciples wonder why this man won the faith award? Were they hurt that Jesus was not as impressed with their faith as with this pagan's? The soldier's faith stood out because it was not in Jesus the man, but in the power of the One who had authorized Him. Not even the disciples had exercised faith from this perspective. They still saw Jesus and themselves as the human source, which is why they often operated in fear and not faith.

Imagine If

If you had been the Roman soldier, would you have been willing for Jesus to declare healing from a distance or would you need Him to come in person? Would you have recognized His power came because of His being under authority? As a disciple, how would you have felt if you knew Jesus singled out someone else's faith? Would you have thought it shocking that Jesus praised the faith of a non-believer? Do you see a difference between your faith and the soldier's? How would you describe the dissimilarity?

PRAYER

Jesus, I want to amaze You with my faith. Teach me how to operate in the same authority You did. I know the Bible says You have given me the same authority and power You had in order for me to do the good works You did of healing the sick, casting out demons and raising the dead. Forgive me for not recognizing the source of my authority. Thank You that I am not under pressure to perform in my own strength. As one under Your authority, I am empowered, like You, to say the words, "Be healed."

· · · · · · · · · · · · · · LOOK UP · · · · · · · · · · · · · ·

Right now you may feel your faith would not astound Jesus. The good news is that you are not expected to live by your faith but by His. Paul told the Galatians we are to live by the faith of the Son of God (see Galatians 2:20). Take your eyes off yourself and set them on Him. He is full of faith for you. During what situations in your life have you seen this the most clearly? Ask Him to speak over your finances, health, family and business. His faith at work will amaze you.

Mystery creates wonder and wonder is the basis of man's desire to *understand.*

—

Neil Armstrong

It Is Never Too Late

> A man named Lazarus was sick. He lived in Bethany with his sisters, Mary and Martha. . . . So the two sisters sent a message to Jesus, telling him, "Lord, your dear friend is very sick." But when Jesus heard about it he said, "Lazarus's sickness will not end in death." So although Jesus loved Martha, Mary, and Lazarus, he stayed where he was for the next two days. Finally he said, "Let's go back to Judea." But his disciples objected. "Rabbi," they said, "only a few days ago the people in Judea were trying to stone you." . . . Then he said, "Our friend Lazarus has fallen asleep, but now I will go and wake him up." . . . When Jesus arrived at Bethany, he was told that Lazarus had already been in his grave for four days. . . . Martha said to Jesus, "Lord, if only you had been here, my brother would not have died." . . . When Mary arrived and saw Jesus, she fell at his feet and said, "Lord, if only you had been here, my brother would not have died." . . . Jesus responded, "Didn't I tell you that you would see God's glory if you believed?"
>
> John 11:1, 3–8, 11, 17, 21, 32, 40

The disciples must have lived in a constant state of surprise. Rarely did their Master act according to logical, obvious, politically or religiously correct norms. Now, even when it involved a dear friend, it appeared He violated His own teaching about friendship. He got word His close friend Lazarus was very ill. Would that not be reason to cancel every engagement to go to Lazarus?

Mary and Martha knew He had healed scores of people, so of course He would come right away and heal their brother no matter what the cost or inconvenience. Without the benefit of a cell phone, they had to wait with no word from Jesus. As the sun set on day one, day two, day three, they watched the life drain out of their brother. Meanwhile the disciples must have wondered, once again, what in the world Jesus was thinking. Time did not seem to matter to Him.

Lazarus' resurrection stunned everyone. As the disciples reflected on the miracle over the next few days, did any of them remember hearing Jesus say His friend was not going to die? Had they not heard Him, or did they misinterpret His meaning? Had they believed Him in the moment but their faith waned as the hours passed? For them, all things were possible but only within a certain time frame. Did this encounter with the supernatural God of time change their thinking?

Imagine If

On what day would you have given up hope? Or would you have expected to see a resurrected body even if it had been eight days and not four? When would your watch have negated the word of God? Would you have doubted Jesus' love for you if He had not come right away? God's love does not always look to us the way it should according to our thinking. Jesus demonstrated His love for them by fulfilling His word to them, not by catering to their emotions. He was not moved by their silent accusations. His love remained constant toward Mary and Martha and toward Lazarus.

PRAYER

O God, forgive me for putting You on the clock. Your Word says, "A day is like a thousand years to the Lord, and a thousand years is like a day" (2 Peter 3:8). Help me to live in Your time zone without becoming impatient. Thank You for Your faithfulness even when my faith wavers as I wait for the fulfillment of Your Word. Thank You for liberation from the tyranny of time. You, and not time, are Lord over all.

· · · · · · · · · · · · · · · · LOOK UP · · · · · · · · · · · · · · · ·

If you are in the waiting room and the situation is critical, the most important action to take right now is to focus your attention on God's love. Remember times when His love comforted you even as the clock was running out. His Word remains true no matter how much time has passed since He spoke it. Do not look at the clock—look at Him. He is not worried or panicked, so you do not need to be either. If at any time He needs you to worry, He will let you know. So for now, be still and know He is Lord over every detail.

Don't let a day pass without being
astonished by something or someone.

—

Marty Rubin

You Get to Choose

Afterward Jesus returned to Jerusalem for one of the Jewish holy days. Inside the city, near the Sheep Gate, was the pool of Bethesda, with five covered porches. Crowds of sick people—blind, lame, or paralyzed—lay on the porches. One of the men lying there had been sick for thirty-eight years. When Jesus saw him and knew he had been ill for a long time, he asked him, "Would you like to get well?" "I can't, sir," the sick man said, "for I have no one to put me into the pool when the water bubbles up. Someone else always gets there ahead of me." Jesus told him, "Stand up, pick up your mat, and walk!" Instantly, the man was healed! He rolled up his sleeping mat and began walking! But this miracle happened on the Sabbath, so the Jewish leaders objected. They said to the man who was cured, "You can't work on the Sabbath! The law doesn't allow you to carry that sleeping mat!" But he replied, "The man who healed me told me, 'Pick up your mat and walk.'" "Who said such a thing as that?" they demanded. The man didn't know, for Jesus had disappeared into the crowd.

John 5:1-13

Did the disabled man think it strange for Jesus to ask him what he wanted? Would it not be obvious? He was not sunbathing by the pool. He had become a fixture there because he needed healing. Was he bitter after years of disappointment? Although he did not give Jesus a direct answer, Jesus discerned by his response that he wanted healing. It was wisdom on Jesus' part to find out if the man wanted healing or pity. Healing his body would not heal his emotional need for pity, which was as crippling as his physical condition. Jesus knew He had power and authority over all disease, but He allowed love to govern His use of it.

The man had spent 38 years dependent on others to help with the simplest tasks, like standing up. Now this stranger told him to stand up. The angel was not there to assist him. The authority of the command must have put life back into his limbs, because he got up. Then Jesus told him to pick up his mat and start walking. Before the man could protest, Jesus' words made the impossible possible. This was not healing by bubbling water but healing by a powerful command. By the time the man had adjusted to his new vertical position, his benefactor had disappeared. What must he have thought that first night, as he lay on his mat no longer disabled after 38 years?

Imagine If

Would you have stood up? What if you had hesitated or said no? Do you think Jesus would have been angry with you? Disappointed? Not at all. Love is kind, not a bully. Kindness gives you permission to make your own decision. Love is patient, allowing you time to come to a decision and to change your mind if you need to. There is no pressure in love, even to receive healing. Isaiah said, "Therefore will the LORD wait, that he may be gracious unto you" (Isaiah 30:18 KJV). And He still waits for you to choose.

PRAYER

Jesus, thank You for demonstrating the Father's wonderful love. Your patience toward me is too much to comprehend. It is hard to believe I am free to take my time to choose. You never try to control me. Forgive me for resisting because I thought You wanted control. I forgive anyone who has tried to control me or portrayed You as a controlling God.

· · · · · · · · · · · · LOOK UP · · · · · · · · · ·

Perhaps you have been dealing with an issue for many years and find it difficult to respond to a command like "stand up." That is okay. Jesus is with you and will help you right where you are. Do you have concerns about what your life will look like on the other side of standing up? Think about what they are, or even write them down. He is willing to sit with you right now and let you process any anxiety, fear or doubt. Remember His love is kind. He has all the time in the world to listen to you; He's not on the clock.

The most beautiful thing we can experience is the *mysterious*. It is the source of all true art and science. He to whom the *emotion* is a stranger, who can no longer pause to wonder and stand wrapped in *awe*, is as good as dead; his eyes are closed.

—

Albert Einstein

Memorable Prayer Meeting

> About eight days later Jesus took Peter, John, and James up on a mountain to pray. And as he was praying, the appearance of his face was transformed, and his clothes became dazzling white. Suddenly two men, Moses and Elijah, appeared and began talking with Jesus. They were glorious to see. And they were speaking about his exodus from this world, which was about to be fulfilled in Jerusalem. Peter and the others had fallen asleep. When they woke up, they saw Jesus' glory and the two men standing with him. As Moses and Elijah were starting to leave, Peter, not even knowing what he was saying, blurted out, "Master, it's wonderful for us to be here! Let's make three shelters as memorials—one for you, one for Moses, and one for Elijah." But even as he was saying this, a cloud overshadowed them, and terror gripped them as the cloud covered them. Then a voice from the cloud said, "This is my Son, my Chosen One. Listen to him." When the voice finished, Jesus was there alone. They didn't tell anyone at that time what they had seen.
>
> Luke 9:28–36

Since we are all supposed to pray, do you think the other disciples wondered why they were not invited to come on the hike? They were still learning the principle of one body with many parts having different functions. Because they were not included in the mission did not mean they were not part of the team.

Meanwhile, the chosen three found themselves in a prayer meeting with Jesus, Moses and Elijah. It was such a momentous experience for them that they all fell asleep. Who falls asleep during such a once-in-a-lifetime experience? Perhaps God put them to sleep so Jesus could have a confidential conversation with Moses and Elijah, just as parents wait for their children to fall asleep before having a private exchange.

<hr />

Once they were awake, the weightiness of the moment sank in. Of course, Peter put forth another one of his brilliant ideas. This time it was to build three memorials—one for Jesus, one for Moses and one for Elijah. His enthusiasm for the project vanished the moment God's voice thundered from the cloud, memorializing the event with a proclamation identifying Jesus as His Son. No building needed.

At that moment, fear overcame them—a holy fear prompted by the mysterious voice of God reverberating above them. Matthew's account of the event reports that they fell facedown on the ground (see Matthew 17:6). One may wonder why they had not fallen on the ground when they saw Jesus transfigured, covered in glory. It is possible they still saw him as a peer rather than the Son of God.

Sometimes it takes a dramatic revelation to put things in proper perspective.

Imagine If

Would you have been jealous of the three? Now picture yourself as part of the chosen. Would you have felt superior because Jesus picked you and not the others? Such a simple scenario as this can reveal so much about how insecure we are with God and with others. When God shows up, everything comes into proper order. We all end up facedown on the ground. Every encounter with God brings more revelation about the nature of God, but also about ourselves. We no longer view God as our buddy. Although we can be intimate with Him, He is still God and we are not. Familiarity with God evaporates as we encounter the God of the cloud.

PRAYER

God, forgive me for any jealousy or superiority I have felt toward others. Thank You that, as Your child, I am already chosen. I am part of Your family and that is enough. Swallow up all of my insecurity in the ocean of Your love. May I always remain in awe of You, never allowing familiarity to creep in to distort my identity in relationship to You. Search my heart. Cleanse me from any arrogance that could rob me of the intimacy I desire.

· · · · · · · · · · · · · · LOOK UP · · · · · · · · · · · · · ·

You may be feeling left out at this moment—or even jealous. Maybe you even need to get facedown. If so, go ahead and do that now. Then set your eyes on Jesus. It is through connection with Him as the Head that we realize we are and always will be one in the Spirit, not because of our superiority but because of His righteousness. We identify with Him in His death, burial and resurrection. Now accepted in the Beloved, we have access to everything for eternity. Pause and give heartfelt thanks for being part of the glorious body of Christ. You belong.

> At moments of wonder, it is easy to avoid small
> thinking, to *entertain* thoughts that span
> the *universe*, that capture both thunder and
> tinkle, thick and thin, the near and the far.
>
> —
>
> Yann Martel

From Doom to Destiny

It was in the year King Uzziah died that I saw the LORD. He was sitting on a lofty throne, and the train of his robe filled the Temple. Attending him were mighty seraphim, each having six wings. With two wings they covered their faces, with two they covered their feet, and with two they flew. They were calling out to each other, "Holy, holy, holy is the LORD of Heaven's Armies!" . . . Their voices shook the Temple to its foundations, and the entire building was filled with smoke. Then I said, "It's all over! I am doomed, for I am a sinful man. I have filthy lips, and I live among a people with filthy lips. Yet I have seen the King, the LORD of Heaven's Armies." Then one of the seraphim flew to me with a burning coal he had taken from the altar with a pair of tongs. He touched my lips with it and said, "See, this coal has touched your lips. Now your guilt is removed, and your sins are forgiven." Then I heard the LORD asking, "Whom should I send as a messenger to this people? Who will go for us?" I said, "Here I am. Send me." And he said, "Yes, go and say to this people."

Isaiah 6:1–9

W hat stunning words: "I saw the Lord." This was not an everyday experience, even for Isaiah the prophet. The fact that the prophet did not immediately prostrate himself is surprising. Did he think this was a dream? But as surreal as it must have felt, God was present in real time, the King of kings seated on His throne, and Isaiah, a mere human, was a witness. His calmness as a spectator quickly changed to fear for his life.

As the building began to shake and smoke filled the Temple, it was too late for Isaiah to evacuate. Would he survive? Either the collapsing building would crush him or the smoke would asphyxiate him. Then the sound of the six-winged angels crying out to each other filled the atmosphere. So far so good. He was still alive. His senses were all buzzing with the sounds, sights and smells around him.

Without warning, an angel took a hot coal from the altar, and as the coal seared his lips, the angel declared him forgiven. Ouch! Although grimacing with pain, he would be thankful to know he was no longer guilty in God's eyes.

As astounding as the encounter with the angels must have been, God's willingness to send him as a messenger might have been even more astonishing. Moments before, he was certain he was going to die. Now God was commissioning him as a missionary. What a stunning turn of events. God does not view our blemished past as a prophecy for our destiny. Those scars are more of an impediment to us than to God. The angels made a point of cleansing the specific area of his life destined to be the instrument of his ministry—his mouth.

Imagine If

Even after the angels purified him and God said, "Go," Isaiah had to receive the forgiveness. If God says *forgiven*, that should settle it. But often it does not. No amount of fire, smoke, angels or even the voice of God can make us accept the pardon. It is staggering to think we would ever dare call God a liar and yet we do any time He says, "Forgiven!" and we respond, "No—guilty!" Would the angel's declaration of forgiveness have convinced you of your freedom from sin? Our past cannot disqualify us unless we allow it to. God qualifies us based on His criteria, not ours.

PRAYER

God, thank You that there is purpose after sin. You are majestic, holy and full of glory and yet willing to send me as Your ambassador. This is sometimes difficult to understand, but I know Your ways and thoughts are not like mine. Show me if I am holding on to any judgment about my past. Today I choose to receive Your forgiveness and step into my destiny.

· · · · · · · · · · · · · · · LOOK UP · · · · · · · · · · · · ·

You may have received forgiveness but still feel bogged down. If so, this would be the perfect time to look up as Isaiah did. Take a moment to see God seated on the throne. Picture the magnificence of His robe filling the Temple. Can you imagine what it would feel like if you brushed up against it? Take a deep breath of the cloud of glorious smoke. In no time the Spirit will lift you up from the bog and seat you with Him in the heavenly place.

Emotion is not simply an *overplus* of feeling; it is life lived at white-heat, the state of wonder. To lose wonder is to lose the true *element* of religion.

—

Oswald Chambers

The Wedding Coordinator

God sent the angel Gabriel to Nazareth, a village in Galilee, to a virgin named Mary. She was engaged to be married. . . . Gabriel appeared to her and said, "Greetings, favored woman! The Lord is with you!" Confused and disturbed, Mary tried to think what the angel could mean. "Don't be afraid, Mary," the angel told her, "for you have found favor with God! You will conceive and give birth to a son, and you will name him Jesus." . . . Mary asked the angel, "But how can this happen? I am a virgin." The angel replied, "The Holy Spirit will come upon you, and the power of the Most High will overshadow you. . . . For the word of God will never fail." Mary responded, "I am the Lord's servant. May everything you have said about me come true."

Luke 1:26-38

Before the marriage took place, while she was still a virgin, [Mary] became pregnant through the power of the Holy Spirit. Joseph, to whom she was engaged, was a righteous man and did not want to disgrace her publicly, so he decided to break the engagement quietly. As he considered this, an angel of the Lord appeared to him in a dream. "Joseph, son of David . . . do not be afraid to take Mary as your wife." . . . When Joseph woke up, he did as the angel of the Lord commanded and took Mary as his wife.

Matthew 1:18-24

When Gabriel greeted her, Mary must have wondered, "Why me?" What had she done to deserve such a startling visitation? Her life at that moment revolved around a marriage, not a baby. What questions would flood her brain all at once? "How can this be?" "What will I tell Joseph?" "Why has God chosen me?" "Will Joseph break the engagement?" "What will God do if I refuse to carry His Son?"

Gabriel did not have to wait long for a response. The reason God chose Mary was because He already knew her heart. He was not gambling. Favor in this moment was not a carrot to bribe her into saying yes; it was the result of years of her yes to His voice.

———————∾———————

Of course, Mary would have been incredulous knowing God dispatched an angel to deliver a message. But the enormity of His request might have been even more astounding. She did not see herself as a person of rank but as a servant of God. What an honor for God to choose her out of all the other women alive on the earth. Would her wonderment have increased when Joseph told her God sent an angel to him as well, telling him to go forward with the marriage? God's concern for the world did not supersede His awareness of her desire to marry Joseph.

Imagine If

What a decision both Mary and Joseph faced. The angel did not give them details for the next nine months. Would Joseph lose his job? Would family and friends shun them? Would you have been willing to say yes if it meant sacrificing the desire of your heart? If you think you would be hesitant, do not condemn yourself. This means you have an opportunity to invite God to reveal more of His loving care to you. Remember, your desires and the little details of your life matter to Him.

PRAYER

God, I want to be able to say yes to You without reservation. Forgive me for any time I have resisted Your invitation because I did not trust You. Jesus said You are aware of even a sparrow falling and that we are of more value than many sparrows (see Matthew 10:31). Thank You for caring about the details of my life as much as the big issues facing the world. Your love continues to amaze me.

· · · · · · · · · · · · · LOOK UP · · · · · · · · · · · · ·

Are you hesitant to say yes to God because of fear that He will not fulfill your dreams? Make a list of every longing of your heart, no matter how small. Then take some time to share these dreams with God. It may surprise you to find that He may have even thought of details you have overlooked. He does not miss a thing when it involves one of His children.

The curse that came before *history* has laid on us all a tendency to be weary of wonders. If we saw the sun for the first time it would be the most fearful and *beautiful* of meteors. Now that we see it for the hundredth time, we call it, in the hideous and blasphemous phrase of Wordsworth, "the *light* of common day."

G. K. Chesterton

Showdown on the Mountain

Ahab went out to meet Elijah. When Ahab saw him, he exclaimed, "So it is really you, you troublemaker of Israel?" "I have made no trouble for Israel," Elijah replied. "You and your family are the troublemakers, for you have refused to obey the commands of the LORD and worshiped the images of Baal instead. Now summon all Israel to join me at Mount Carmel, along with the 450 prophets of Baal and 400 prophets of Asherah who are supported by Jezebel." . . . Then Elijah stood in front of them and said, "How much longer will you waver, hobbling between two opinions? If the LORD is God, follow him! But if Baal is God, then follow him!" But the people were completely silent. . . . At the usual time for offering the evening sacrifice, Elijah prayed, "O LORD God, prove today that you are God and that I am your servant. . . . O LORD, answer me . . . so these people will know that you, O LORD, are God and that you have brought them back to yourself." Immediately the fire of the LORD flashed down from heaven and burned up the young bull, the wood, the stones. . . . And when the people saw it, they fell face down on the ground and cried out, "The LORD—he is God!"

1 Kings 18:16-21, 36-39

Elijah's challenge to the prophets of Baal was a bold move. It is possible they had never been in a situation where they had to depend on their god. Elijah had the okay from his God. Was Baal agreeable to this showdown with Elijah's God? Why were the prophets so silent when Elijah asked them to verbalize their allegiance? Were they wondering if their god was behind them, or were they terrified he would abandon them?

They soon discovered the answer to that. They screamed to their god for hours. Begging him to send fire on their offering. Nothing. Would Elijah's God answer him? Was Elijah sweating at all as his turn came? Even if he felt he had God's endorsement, there might have been a moment of anxiety as he faced 850 hostile prophets, eager to rid their nation of this troublemaker.

•————————∽————————•

When God showed up, it might have literally taken their breath away. You can almost hear the fire as it swooshed down from heaven and consumed the bull, the wood and even the water in the trench around the altar. Elijah did not need to take a poll on who was the true God. Their immediate facedown posture told him their vote. If God decides to show Himself as the consuming fire, it is hard to remain a skeptic about His Lordship. But usually He would rather woo us with the fire of His love than intimidate us with His blazing firepower.

Imagine It

How would you have felt if you had been Elijah's assistant, arranging the wood and placing the bull on the altar? Would you have thought he was being a little arrogant? Should he dial down his rhetoric a bit? Or would his boldness have been contagious, stirring you to new levels of faith in God? Courageous faith not only makes believers out of non-believers but also can make weak believers strong. Elijah is not meant to be the only example of a daring believer in God's hall of heroes. God invites us to take our place alongside Elijah and all the other righteous men and women who were bold as lions on earth.

PRAYER

God, fill me with the same Spirit Elijah had. I want the baptism of fire in my life so non-believers encounter You through me and fall facedown in Your presence. Forgive me for the times I have shrunk back in fear of confrontation. I want to be a faithful witness for You in any situation. Thank You for the gift of Your righteousness. I depend on it as the source of my courage, rather than my own. You make me brave.

· · · · · · · · · · · · · · · · # LOOK UP · · · · · · · · · · · · · · · ·

If you are facing an Ahab situation right now, take heart, knowing that you have this because God has you. He did not let Elijah down, and He will not abandon you either. The Spirit in you is not afraid of the conflict. He is your strength. God is King of kings and Lord of lords. Think of a time when He came through for you when it seemed like there was no way ahead, and remind yourself of that time whenever you feel overwhelmed. He is ready to show off for you in any showdown.

You will never *cease* to be the most amazed person on earth at what God has done for you on the *inside*.

—

Oswald Chambers

An Extraordinary Victory

Messengers came and told Jehoshaphat, "A vast army from Edom is marching against you from beyond the Dead Sea. They are already at Hazazon-tamar." . . . Jehoshaphat was terrified by this news and begged the LORD for guidance. He also ordered everyone in Judah to begin fasting. So people from all the towns of Judah came to Jerusalem to seek the LORD's help. Jehoshaphat stood before the community . . . and . . . prayed . . . "O our God, won't you stop them? We are powerless against this mighty army. . . . We do not know what to do, but we are looking to you for help." . . . "This is what the LORD says: Do not be afraid! Don't be discouraged for the battle is not yours, but God's. . . . You will not even need to fight. Take your positions; then stand still and watch the LORD's victory." . . . Then King Jehoshaphat bowed low with his face to the ground. And all the people did the same, worshiping the LORD. . . . Early the next morning the army went out. . . . The king appointed singers to walk ahead of the army. . . . At the very moment they began to sing . . . the LORD caused the armies . . . to start fighting among themselves. . . . So when the army of Judah arrived at the lookout point . . . all they saw were dead bodies lying on the ground as far as they could see.

2 Chronicles 20:2-24

Jehoshaphat, although a battle-tested king, knew he needed a strategy from God to conquer the army heading toward him. This was a terrifying situation for him as well as the people. In desperation they sought God with prayer and fasting. The king needed God to give him a battle plan. There was none. Jehoshaphat must have been incredulous when God told them the plan was to take their place and stand still. Stand still in the face of a militant army arrayed in battle dress ready to annihilate them all? He might not have said it, but he might have thought to himself, "God, You are crazy! We are all going to die. No one stands still in front of their enemy and survives."

•————⌒————•

God did not instruct Jehoshaphat to send the worship band in front of the army; he did that on his own. Was he thinking it would have an effect on the enemy? Was it to keep the army focused on God, as they were about to die? Or was he worshiping in anticipation of a miraculous deliverance from God as the Lord of heaven's army? It might have been a mix of fear and faith. But there must have been a gasp as they reached the lookout point, expecting to see thousands of bodies in battle stance, only to see dead bodies strewn over the ground into the distance. What an extraordinary God!

Imagine If

Would your voice have quavered if you were one of the singers? What would your expectation have been? Victory or obliteration? This might have been the moment you took a leap of faith and believed God. Why not? Better to die in peace than in fear. Would you have tried to remember all the past eleventh-hour impossible victories when all you could do was stand still and hope God would show up?

PRAYER

God, thank You for every time You came through for me. Who knows, would I even be here today if You had not? You have astounded me with Your ability to save me from certain death or destruction. How could I ever doubt You? And yet I do sometimes. Forgive me for giving in to fear because You told me to stand still. It is so much easier to do something rather than nothing. Help me to see You working as I am watching.

· · · · · · · · · · · LOOK UP · · · · · · · · · · ·

If you are struggling to remain calm in a battle, be still for a minute. There is great benefit to being quiet. God told David to "be still, and know that I am God" (Psalm 46:10). Write this verse (or another verse that speaks to you) on paper and post it where you will see it, like on the bathroom mirror. Ask the Holy Spirit right now to calm your anxious mind and racing heart. Now listen for His whisper to stand still as you watch Him fight for you.

It should be expected that we will find wonder in a vast mountain *landscape,* but it is a more serious challenge to find wonder in a hill. It is a great *achievement* to find it in a molehill.

—

Tristan Gooley

Remarkable Family Ties

> As Jesus was speaking to the crowd, his mother and brothers stood outside, asking to speak to him. Someone told Jesus, "Your mother and your brothers are outside, and they want to speak to you." Jesus asked, "Who is my mother? Who are my brothers? . . . Anyone who does the will of my Father in heaven is my brother and sister and mother!"
>
> Matthew 12:46–50

> Standing near the cross were Jesus' mother, and his mother's sister, Mary (the wife of Clopas), and Mary Magdalene. When Jesus saw his mother standing there beside the disciple he loved, he said to her, "Dear woman, here is your son." And he said to this disciple, "Here is your mother." And from then on this disciple took her into his home.
>
> John 19:25–27

In the Jewish culture, your family lineage was part of your identity. Even if your family tree had several bad apples, they remained in the family pedigree. That is the reason the Old Testament writers did not rewrite history by deleting certain undesirables. This emphasis on family originated with God, the source of family. He also established the first adoption program, fulfilling His desire for children. Jesus' mission was to reveal the Father to the world as well as enable restoration to God's family.

God also provided the first book on family life. He commanded children to honor their fathers and mothers, even the imperfect ones. Obedience to that command resulted in the child being blessed with a good long life (see Ephesians 6:1–3). Did the disciples worry that Jesus was dishonoring His mother when He did not immediately respond to her request to speak with Him? Jesus of all people should have shown the deepest respect to Mary, but He did not seem to in this situation.

Jesus not only knew the Word; He was the Word. Everything that came out of His mouth would have had an element of revelation because God's thoughts filled His mind. The disciples lived 24/7 in mind-renewal training both of the ways and also the mindsets of God revealed to them by Jesus. Did they ever want to call a time-out to process some of these mind-boggling perspectives? In this case, as they were about to pull Jesus aside to remind Him about honoring His mother, He opened their minds to the kingdom perspective on family ties. In the kingdom, love for the Father expressed by doing His will determines family relationship, not one's DNA. This revelation might have left them shaking their heads in wonder.

Imagine If

Would you have wanted to whisper in Jesus' ear to make sure He knew His mother wanted Him? Or would you have pulled a brash Peter move and called Him out for His rudeness to her? How would you have felt if you had no family and heard Jesus' explanation of what constituted family ties? Would you have seen the believers around you through this new lens? What about some who were less mature but were still followers of Jesus? How would this revelation affect your attitude toward them? Family is not always convenient. It may mean having one of those immature believers in your home, or an older person who might require more care, like Mary.

PRAYER

God, thank You that I am invited to be part of Your family through adoption. I know that sometimes I have not accepted some family members because they do not look like me, vote like I do or pray the same. But they love You and serve You the best they know how. Please forgive me for my unkindness toward them. Help me open my heart and embrace all our family, even if it is costly or inconvenient.

· · · · · · · · · · · · · · LOOK UP · · · · · · · · · · · · · ·

Do you feel alone today? Have you lost a family member or friend? Or are you in a new location separated from your relatives? Are you the only believer in your immediate family right now? If so, do not despair. Your Father knows your need for a family as Jesus knew His mother's. Talk to Him right now. Ask Him to give you peace, and to bring other Christians into your life. In the meantime, He as your Father is able to fill the emptiness with His marvelous presence, and He will connect you with others in His family. You are not destined to be alone forever.

One must not fear to be a little *child* again,
when times of wonder are at hand.

—

Jody Lynn Nye

Off the Hook

> On their arrival in Capernaum, the collectors of the Temple tax came to Peter and asked him, "Doesn't your teacher pay the Temple tax?" "Yes, He does," Peter replied. Then he went into the house. But before he had a chance to speak, Jesus asked him, "What do you think, Peter? Do kings tax their own people or the people they have conquered?" "They tax the people they have conquered," Peter replied. "Well, then," Jesus said, "the citizens are free! However, we don't want to offend them, so go down to the lake and throw in a line. Open the mouth of the first fish you catch, and you will find a large silver coin. Take it and pay the tax for both of us."
>
> Matthew 17:24–27

Matthew is the only gospel writer who reports this event. The story may have caught his attention as a temple-tax-paying Jew and former tax collector. Not too long before this event, Jesus' magnetic call to join the team had interrupted Matthew's day job in Capernaum. Peter was the only disciple involved in the story, but he must have shared it with Matthew.

By this time in Peter's discipleship training, he had seen the feeding of the five thousand, the feeding of the four thousand, physical healings, supernatural storm control, a

demonized boy set free and most recently the transfiguration of Jesus. Life on the road with Jesus must have been
like running with Superman—exhilarating but exhausting.

Peter had recently experienced a stinging public rebuke
from Jesus. No one wanted to be humiliated by the Teacher
in front of peers. One minute he was singled out for recognizing Jesus as Messiah. The next moment Jesus responded
to his comment with "Get behind me, Satan!" (see Matthew
16:13–23).

Experiencing physical, mental and spiritual overload, he
might not have had time to process all these events before
fielding a question about Jesus' tax payments. He was a
fisherman, not a CPA, but answered on Jesus' behalf. Did
he know what to say because he and Jesus had talked about
taxes, or was this another off-the-cuff response he would
later regret? He was not wealthy, nor was he the treasurer of
the group, yet he assured the tax collector that Jesus would
pay. This yearly tax was not exorbitant, but their ministry
was not flush with honorariums and had no books to sell.
Did he realize what he had done?

————————∽————————

As Peter walked into the house, did he have the fleeting
thought, "What will I tell Jesus about the taxes?" Was he
holding his breath, waiting for Jesus to correct him for
overstepping his authority? Or had Peter figured out how
he would get the money for the tax? Had he stepped into a

new level of faith, remembering Jesus had said not to worry about life since His Father knows what we need and all the silver and gold are His (see Matthew 6:31–32; Haggai 2:8)?

Jesus confronted the tax issue head-on even though He had been inside, out of earshot of the conversation. This was not the first time Jesus demonstrated supernatural knowledge. Peter escaped correction for possibly overstepping his authority this time. Was his relief over no rebuke from Jesus so great that it overshadowed any hesitation to follow Jesus' direction to catch a fish and pull a coin out of its mouth to pay the tax for both of them? Sometimes finding ourselves off the hook is more awesome than the challenge to hook a fish with a coin in its mouth.

Imagine If

Have you ever been in a situation where you said or did something that could have painful, embarrassing, expensive repercussions? What did you feel when you realized what you had done and knew you had to face your boss, spouse, pastor, parent or God? Dread? Fear? Panic? Or was your experience all of the above? If you received a merciful response, did you feel wonder-filled relief to be off the hook?

PRAYER

Father, thank You that even when I display my clay feet, and may have put them in my mouth, You have pity on me. Your mercy wrecks me. Nothing I do is beyond Your bank of possibilities, even if it means sending me to fish for silver coins. The wonder of a Father like You who does not condemn, but comes alongside to help me, is overwhelming.

LOOK UP

You may have pulled a Peter and spent a restless night in dread of the outcome. This is your opportunity to take a minute right now to experience a mercy miracle. Look for it. Listen for it. Live today in the relief of it. In what situation do you need to get your fishing pole and go fish for whatever coin you need to resolve the issue? Remember, God has a fish for you with a coin in its mouth.

It's tough to have an *authentic* relationship with awe in the age of *awesome*, a word that has become so overused as to be drained of its meaning.

—

Sharon Salzberg

The Master Chef

Simon Peter said, "I'm going fishing." "We'll come, too," they all said. So they went out in the boat, but they caught nothing all night. At dawn Jesus was standing on the beach, but the disciples couldn't see who he was. He called out, "Fellows, have you caught any fish?" "No," they replied. Then he said, "Throw out your net on the right-hand side of the boat, and you'll get some!" So they did, and they couldn't haul in the net because there were so many fish in it. Then the disciple Jesus loved said to Peter, "It's the Lord!" When Peter heard that it was the Lord, he jumped into the water, and headed to the shore. The others stayed with the boat and pulled the loaded net to the shore. When they got there, they found breakfast waiting for them—fish cooking over a charcoal fire, and some bread. "Bring some of the fish you've just caught," Jesus said. . . . "Now come and have some breakfast!" . . . None of the disciples dared to ask him, "Who are you?" They knew it was the Lord. Then Jesus served them the bread and the fish.

John 21:3-13

Peter and his friends, reeling from the cruel death of their Master, must have wondered how they could bear the loss of not only their friend but the leader of their movement. They spent three years learning about a new world order, watching demonstrations of supernatural power that caused the masses to look to Jesus as a possible king. What had become of the vision of a kingdom on earth? It is unlikely there was discussion that night about who was the greatest or who would get the best seat. A kingdom needs a king, and He was dead.

Peter decided to try to soothe his anger, grief and confusion by returning to what he knew best—fishing. No consolation there. Not one fish to show for his work. Had life on the road dulled his fishing skill? It probably appeared to him that he had lost not only his job in the ministry but also his fallback livelihood as a fisherman. What a hopeless situation.

Our despair is often what God is waiting for. He is the physician for the sick, the deliverer for the bound, the comforter for the grieving, peace for the storm-tossed and hope for the hopeless. If we had heard Peter's response to the man's inquiry, would the tone of his *no* have revealed the depth of his pain? Then the man told him to throw the net out on the other side. This time, Peter was so numb he did not argue. And once again, Jesus knew where the fish would be. Peter's moment of awe might not have been the fish eyes staring at him from the net but the eyes of his resurrected Master calling to him from shore. Once he reached the beach, he was in for another stunning moment as Jesus, his Master, served him breakfast as a Master chef.

Imagine It

Could you feel the roller coaster of emotions Peter experienced? Would you have been as down in the dumps as Peter was? When you heard the voice from shore suggesting you throw your nets on the other side, would you have remembered the earlier catch that almost sank the boat? Would the amazement of the moment have inspired you to run across the water? Is it hard to picture Jesus, the King, doing something as mundane as grilling fish for you? He told the disciples that He came to serve, and He did. It is often easier to accept His sacrifice on the cross than His service in the mundane.

PRAYER

Jesus, You continue to surprise me. The picture of You cooking breakfast reveals another facet of Your desire to be part of my life. The more I know about You, the more I love You. Forgive me for the times I thought You were too busy on important matters to eat breakfast with me. I realize You are as interested in feeding me as in saving me. You want to meet all my needs—body, soul and spirit.

· · · · · · · · · · · · · · · **LOOK UP** · · · · · · · · · · · · · · ·

Have you been walking through disappointment, disillusion-
ment or loss? Have you tried to find solace without success?
Rest assured that He is as present today, ready to serve you,
as He was when cooking breakfast on the beach for the disciples. Take a moment and listen. He's calling to you, "Breakfast is ready. Come and eat what I have prepared for you."
Run to Him. Do not let the food get cold!

There are only two ways to live your life. One
is as though nothing is a *miracle*. The other
is as though *everything* is a miracle.

—

Anonymous

Acknowledgments

Thank you to all my family and friends who have encouraged me with their words, prayers and coffee dates throughout this project. And thank you to David Sluka and the Chosen Books team for the opportunity to work with you again.

FAITH BLATCHFORD serves at Bethel Church in Redding, California, as a pastoral counselor and travels around the world from there as a conference speaker, teaching on various topics, including the prophetic, spiritual warfare, dreams and unlocking creative potential. She is also a regional facilitator-at-large of the International Bethel Sozo ministry. Her desire is to help people encounter the presence of God.

Faith says she was born a "Navy brat," but then her dad became an Episcopal priest, making her a PK (preacher's kid) instead. Although her mother sometimes called her a "handful," she says neither the Navy nor the Church was to blame! When she was eight, her dad was diagnosed with cancer and sought both medical treatment and divine healing. As a result, Faith had her first encounter with God at a healing service she attended with her parents. Since that experience, she has had a hunger for more of the presence of God. (And yes, her father was healed.)

Faith majored in religion at a secular college (not the easiest thing, she says) and wrote her senior thesis on "The Challenge of Twentieth-Century Divine Healing." She has been in ministry ever since graduation and has served in various places, including a retreat center, some churches and a Christian school. For more information on her ministry and available resources, visit her online at www.faith blatchford.com.